CATECHISM
OF THE
SEVEN SACRAMENTS

KEVIN AND MARY O'NEILL

BUILDING BLOCKS OF FAITH SERIES

SOPHIA INSTITUTE PRESS
Manchester, New Hampshire

Sophia Institute Press
Box 5284, Manchester, NH 03108
1-800-888-9344
www.SophiaInstitute.com

Sophia Institute Press® is a registered trademark of Sophia Institute.

hardcover ISBN 978-1-64413-732-1
ebook ISBN 978-1-64413-733-8

Library of Congress Control Number: 2022947353

MANY THANKS, ESPECIALLY TO:

Our dedicated team of editors: Donna-Marie Frommeyer and Bridget Wedoff. As well as editorial assistance from Matt and Sarah Ann Doetsch, Paul and Jeanette Doetsch, Tom and Magdalena Hudson, Luke and Renee Kehoe, Cynthia Martinez, The Masterson Family, Mary Smith, and Marilyn Weadon.

Prayers and theological review and support from The Canons Regular of Saint John Cantius, especially Rev. Anthony Rice S.J.C. and Rev. Nathan Caswell S.J.C., as well as Rev. John McNamara.

Creative set inspirations by our team of builders, our children: Madelyn, Colin, Liam, Brigid, Molly, Moira, and Fulton O'Neill, as well as our guest builders: Zack Kendall, Gabriel Lugo, and Andrew Smith.

TABLE OF CONTENTS

INTRODUCTION

I often say that, as Catholics, we read the Bible in 3-D. This is because our faith comes alive through Sacred Scripture, Sacred Tradition, and the Magisterium of the Catholic Church. Never while saying this did it ever occur to me that someday I would combine those same 3-D biblical teachings with fun 3-D images to help teach the beauty of the faith in a simple way. Using these fun images alongside precise Catholic terminology, this book is a theological work aimed to both entertain and teach a broad audience. This book is for everyone — from 0 years old to 120 years old.

After falling in love with the beauty of the Bride of Christ, the Church, my wife Mary and I want to help others discover that same beauty. Where better to begin than the sacraments! Since the fall of mankind, sin has separated humanity from God. Christ instituted the sacraments to reunite humanity with God. We explain the sacraments by starting with the New and Everlasting Covenant, the Holy Eucharist. Every sacrament both stems from and points to the Holy Eucharist — the source and summit of our Catholic faith.

This book follows Pope Emeritus Benedict XVI's teaching on Theology of Covenant, which is a framework for interpreting Scripture centered on Christ, grounded in the unity of the entire Bible. Theology of Covenant is said to be the master key to unlock the biblical understanding of salvation history.

While telling this story of salvation history through scriptural teachings of the sacraments, we make use of typology, one of the best ways to teach the faith and a favorite tool of Venerable Archbishop Fulton J. Sheen. Typology is a method of biblical study in which elements found in the Old Testament are shown to prefigure those found in the New Testament. As you read, you will see biblical typology unlocked with memorable side-by-side building block illustrations that show how the Old is fulfilled in the New and the New is revealed in the Old.

We consider ourselves to be products of Pope St. John Paul II's New Evangelization, learning and building our faith through all types of media. Now, through the Building Blocks of Faith Series, we hope to contribute to the New Evangelization by helping to catechise and evangelize others. After spending nearly two years writing this book and building the illustrations as a family, we are excited and humbled to be able to share it with you and your family!

—Kevin O'Neill

THE EUCHARIST

WAIT A MINUTE. WHAT IS A PASSOVER?
TO EXPLAIN THE PASSOVER, WE HAVE TO GO BACK THOUSANDS OF YEARS BEFORE JESUS. THE FIRST PASSOVER HAPPENED DURING THE TIME OF MOSES AND PHARAOH ...
POOF!
983
1510
1820
1985

AFTER MOSES DEFENDED AN ISRAELITE, HE FLED FROM EGYPT.

MOSES WAS AN ISRAELITE BY BIRTH, BUT HE WAS RAISED AS AN EGYPTIAN PRINCE.

GOD LOVED THE ISRAELITES. HE APPEARED TO MOSES AND TOLD HIM TO DELIVER A MESSAGE TO PHARAOH: "LET MY PEOPLE GO TO WORSHIP ME!"

EX 2:1-4, EX 2:15, EX 9:1

DURING THE FIRST PLAGUE, THE NILE RIVER TURNED TO BLOOD.

THE SECOND PLAGUE BROUGHT FROGS.

EX 7:20, EX 8:1-4

THE THIRD PLAGUE BROUGHT BUGS AND LICE.

AND THE FOURTH PLAGUE BROUGHT WILD ANIMALS AND FLIES.

THE FIFTH PLAGUE WAS DISEASED LIVESTOCK.

THE SIXTH PLAGUE WAS BOILS.

THE SEVENTH PLAGUE BROUGHT HAIL AND FIRE.

THE EIGHTH PLAGUE WAS LOCUSTS.

THE NINTH PLAGUE WAS DARKNESS FOR THREE DAYS.

AND THEN CAME THE TENTH PLAGUE. MOSES TOLD PHARAOH THAT IF HE DID NOT LISTEN TO GOD, ALL OF EGYPT'S FIRSTBORN SONS WOULD DIE. BUT PHARAOH'S HEART WAS HARDENED, AND HE WOULD NOT LISTEN.

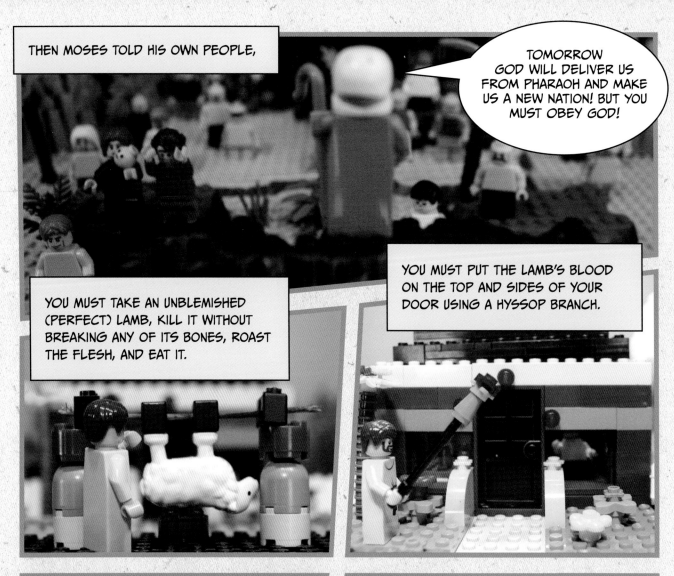

THEN MOSES TOLD HIS OWN PEOPLE,

TOMORROW GOD WILL DELIVER US FROM PHARAOH AND MAKE US A NEW NATION! BUT YOU MUST OBEY GOD!

YOU MUST TAKE AN UNBLEMISHED (PERFECT) LAMB, KILL IT WITHOUT BREAKING ANY OF ITS BONES, ROAST THE FLESH, AND EAT IT.

YOU MUST PUT THE LAMB'S BLOOD ON THE TOP AND SIDES OF YOUR DOOR USING A HYSSOP BRANCH.

YOU MUST MAKE BREAD THAT IS UNLEAVENED (NO YEAST).

YOU MUST EAT STANDING UP AND BE READY TO LEAVE!

EX 12:3, EX 12:5, EX 12:22, EX 12:19, EX 12:11

THE ISRAELITES OBEYED GOD, SO THE ANGEL OF DEATH "PASSED OVER" THEIR HOUSES.

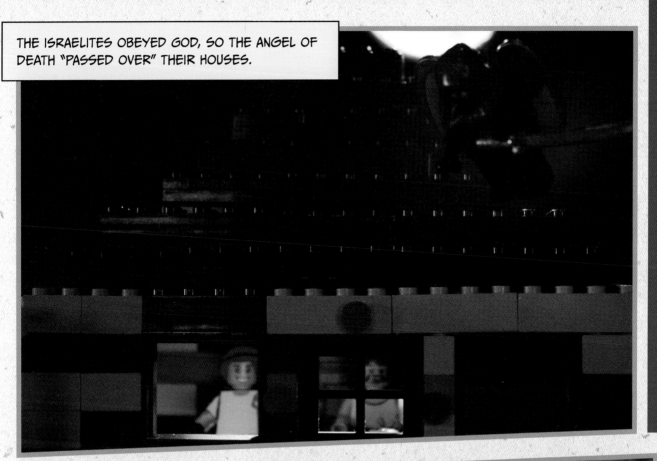

BUT THE EGYPTIANS DID NOT OBEY GOD. SO ALL OF THEIR FIRSTBORN SONS DIED, INCLUDING PHARAOH'S OWN SON.

EX 12:23, EX 12:30

BUT PHARAOH WAS ANGRY! EVEN THOUGH HE TOLD THEM TO LEAVE, HE AND HIS ARMY CHASED AFTER THEM.

GOD DELIVERED HIS PEOPLE, THE ISRAELITES, THROUGH THE RED SEA.

BUT PHARAOH AND HIS ARMY WERE OVERTHROWN.

SO THE ISRAELITES WERE BORN A NEW NATION, WITH MOSES LEADING THEM AND GOD DELIVERING THEM FROM SLAVERY AND BONDAGE THROUGH THEIR OBEDIENCE DURING THE FIRST PASSOVER.

EX 14:30-31

NOW I GET IT! THE PASSOVER IS WHEN THE ANGEL OF DEATH "PASSED OVER" THE HOUSES OF THE PEOPLE WHO OBEYED GOD.

BUT WHAT I STILL DON'T UNDERSTAND IS: WHAT DOES THE PASSOVER, WHICH HAPPENED THOUSANDS OF YEARS AGO, HAVE TO DO WITH CHRIST AND THE LAST SUPPER?

EVERY YEAR, THE ISRAELITES AND ALL OF THEIR DESCENDANTS WERE INSTRUCTED TO KEEP THE FEAST OF THE PASSOVER. THIS WAS TO REMEMBER THEIR TIME IN SLAVERY AND BONDAGE AND TO THANK GOD FOR DELIVERING THEM AND MAKING THEM A NEW NATION.

EX 12:14

29

THE PASSOVER MEAL, ALTHOUGH IT IS ONE MEAL, IS DIVIDED INTO FOUR CUPS.

THE FIRST CUP IS THE CUP OF **SANCTIFICATION**. IT REPRESENTS THE ISRAELITES' BITTER TIME IN SLAVERY AND BONDAGE. DURING THIS CUP THEY EAT BITTER HERBS AND SPICES.

THE SECOND CUP IS THE CUP OF **PROCLAMATION**. IT REPRESENTS THE ISRAELITES LEAVING EGYPT. DURING THIS CUP THEY TELL THE STORY OF THE ISRAELITES' EXIT FROM EGYPT.

AFTER THE FIRST CUP, A HYMN IS SUNG.

THE THIRD CUP IS THE CUP OF **BLESSING**. IT REPRESENTS THE ISRAELITES BEING DELIVERED THROUGH THE RED SEA. DURING THIS CUP THEY EAT THE SACRIFICED LAMB AND THE UNLEAVENED BREAD.

THE FOURTH CUP IS THE CUP OF **PRAISE**. IT REPRESENTS THE ISRAELITES BECOMING A NEW NATION.

AFTER THE THIRD CUP, A HYMN IS SUNG AGAIN.

AFTER THE FOURTH CUP OF THE PASSOVER IS CONSUMED ... **IT IS FINISHED!**

EX 6:6, EX 6:6, EX 6:6, EX 6:7

AFTER GOD DELIVERED MOSES AND HIS PEOPLE FROM EGYPT, GOD TOLD MOSES THAT HE WOULD RAISE UP A PROPHET JUST LIKE HIM.

THAT PROPHET IS JESUS!

LK 22:15, DEU 18:15-19

THERE ARE MANY SIMILARITIES BETWEEN CHRIST AND MOSES.

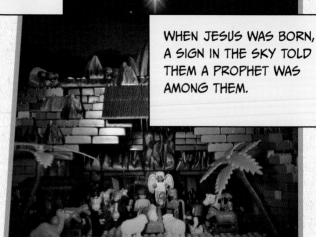

WHEN JESUS WAS BORN, A SIGN IN THE SKY TOLD THEM A PROPHET WAS AMONG THEM.

WHEN MOSES WAS BORN, A SIGN IN THE SKY TOLD THEM A PROPHET WAS AMONG THEM.

WHEN MOSES WAS BORN, PHARAOH SENT OUT AN EDICT (ORDER) TO HAVE ALL THE YOUNG BOYS KILLED SO HE COULD KILL THE PROPHET.

WHEN JESUS WAS BORN, HEROD SENT OUT AN EDICT TO HAVE ALL THE YOUNG BOYS KILLED SO HE COULD KILL THE PROPHET.

MOSES WAS SENT DOWN THE RIVER INTO THE HEART OF EGYPT TO ESCAPE PHARAOH'S WRATH.

JESUS, MARY, AND JOSEPH FLED INTO THE HEART OF EGYPT TO ESCAPE HEROD'S WRATH.

MAT 2:2, EX 1:22, MAT 2:16, EX 2:3, MAT 2:13

MOSES WAS THE PRINCE OF EGYPT, WHO STEPPED OUT OF HIS KINGDOM TO BE WITH HIS PEOPLE AND LEAD THEM OUT OF SLAVERY THROUGH A PASSOVER MEAL.

JESUS IS THE PRINCE OF PEACE, WHO STEPPED OUT OF HIS KINGDOM TO BE WITH HIS PEOPLE AND LEAD THEM OUT OF THE SLAVERY OF SIN THROUGH FULFILLING THE PASSOVER MEAL.

MOSES' FIRST PUBLIC MIRACLE WAS TURNING THE RIVER TO BLOOD.

CHRIST'S FIRST PUBLIC MIRACLE WAS TURNING THE WATER INTO WINE AT THE WEDDING FEAST AT CANA. LATER HE CHANGED WINE INTO HIS BLOOD AT THE PASSOVER HE CELEBRATED THE NIGHT BEFORE HE DIED.

THIS BRINGS US BACK TO THE LAST SUPPER WITH CHRIST AND HIS DISCIPLES—MY FAVORITE SACRAMENT!

EX 2:10, ISA 9:6, EX 7:19, JN 2:9, MAT 26:18

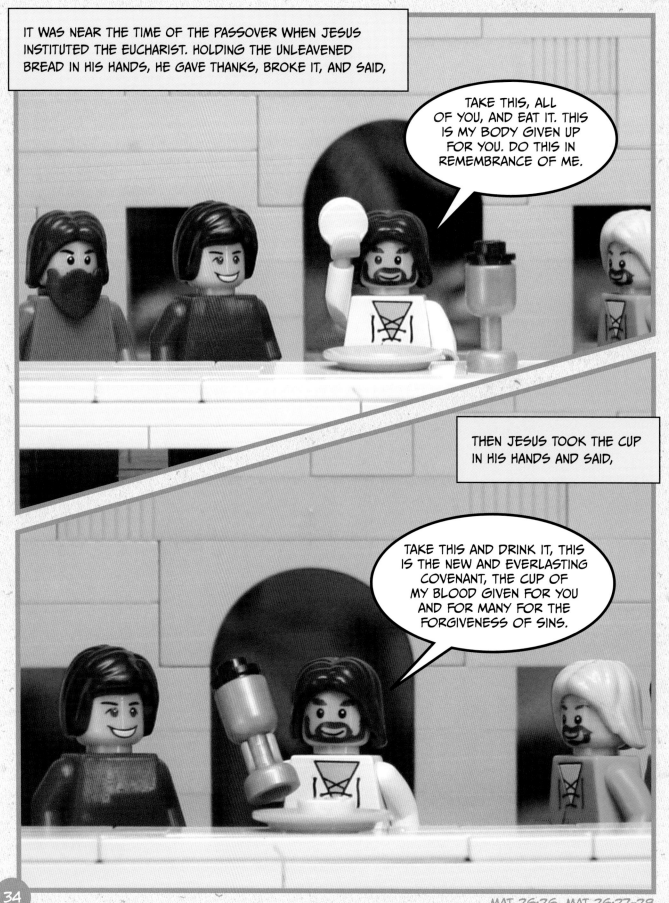

AFTER JESUS DID THIS, HE SAID,

THEN THEY SANG A HYMN, AND, NOT FINISHING THE FOURTH CUP OF THE PASSOVER, WENT INTO THE GARDEN OF GETHSEMANE.

I WILL NOT DRINK OF THE FRUIT OF THE VINE AGAIN UNTIL I ENTER MY FATHER'S KINGDOM.

IN THE GARDEN JESUS SAID,

FATHER, IF IT IS POSSIBLE, LET THIS CUP PASS, BUT LET NOT MY WILL, BUT YOUR WILL, BE DONE.

WHILE JESUS WAS PRAYING IN THE GARDEN, HE KNEW HE WOULD HAVE TO FINISH THE PASSOVER ON THE CROSS.

MAT 26:29, MAT 26:30; MAT 26:39, MAT 26:40

HE WAS, HOWEVER, PUNISHED ANYWAY.

HE WAS BEATEN, LED TO THE CROSS, AND EVEN NAILED TO THE CROSS. YET NO BONES WERE BROKEN, JUST LIKE THE PASSOVER LAMB.

INRI

WHEN HE WAS ON THE CROSS, HE SAID, "I THIRST." THE GUARD TOOK A SPONGE SOAKED IN WINE AND PUT IT ON A HYSSOP BRANCH.

INRI

REMEMBER, THE HYSSOP BRANCH IS THE SAME BRANCH THE ISRAELITES USED TO PUT THE LAMB'S BLOOD ON THE DOOR DURING THE FIRST PASSOVER.

THEN CHRIST DRANK IT AND SAID,

IT IS FINISHED.

INRI

HE ALSO WANTS US TO RECEIVE HIM. THAT IS WHY HE INSTITUTED THE EUCHARIST AT THE LAST SUPPER.

WHEN WE RECEIVE THE HOLY EUCHARIST, WE ARE RECEIVING JESUS. WE ARE EATING THE PASSOVER LAMB!

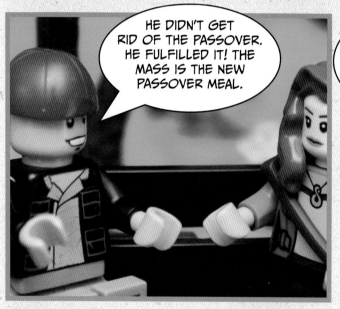

HE DIDN'T GET RID OF THE PASSOVER. HE FULFILLED IT! THE MASS IS THE NEW PASSOVER MEAL.

IN FACT, JESUS, WHO IS GOD, ONLY SAID THE WORD "COVENANT" ONE TIME.

RIGHT, AT THE LAST SUPPER, BUT WHAT IS A COVENANT?

A COVENANT IS AN AGREEMENT BETWEEN GOD AND HIS PEOPLE.

GOD HAS ALWAYS ESTABLISHED A COVENANT WITH HIS PEOPLE. IF YOU WERE OUTSIDE OF THE COVENANT, YOU WERE OUTSIDE OF THE FAMILY OF GOD.

MAT 26:17-30, 1 COR 5:7, 1 COR 5:7-8, LK 22:20, CCC 1150, EPH 2:12

IN THE **FIRST COVENANT**, ADAM AND EVE WERE MADE FOR EACH OTHER AND GIVEN TO EACH OTHER IN MARRIAGE. GOD COMMANDED THEM TO BE FRUITFUL AND MULTIPLY.

GEN 1:28

IN THE **SECOND COVENANT**, NOAH AND HIS FAMILY (EIGHT IN ALL), PLUS SEVEN PAIRS OF THE CLEAN ANIMALS AND ONE PAIR OF THE UNCLEAN ANIMALS, WERE SAVED FROM THE FLOOD THAT COVERED THE WHOLE EARTH. AFTER THE FLOOD, GOD COMMANDED THEM TO BE FRUITFUL AND MULTIPLY.

IN THE **THIRD COVENANT**, GOD CALLED ABRAM AND GAVE HIM THE NAME ABRAHAM, WHICH MEANS, "THE FATHER OF A MULTITUDE OF NATIONS." GOD PROMISED TO MAKE HIM THE FATHER OF A GREAT NATION WITH DESCENDANTS AS NUMEROUS AS THE STARS.

THE **FOURTH COVENANT** IS WHEN GOD CHOSE MOSES TO LEAD HIS PEOPLE OUT OF SLAVERY TO THE PROMISED LAND. HE GAVE THEM THE TEN COMMANDMENTS. ALSO, THE LEVITICAL PRIESTHOOD WAS ESTABLISHED.

IN THE **FIFTH COVENANT**, DAVID, A SHEPHERD BOY, BECAME THE KING OF ISRAEL. GOD PROMISED HIM AN HEIR WHO WOULD BUILD GOD'S TEMPLE, BE THE SON OF GOD, AND RULE OVER JERUSALEM FOREVER.

AND FINALLY, **THE NEW AND EVERLASTING COVENANT** IS THE EUCHARIST! JESUS CAME TO FULFILL ALL OF THE OLD COVENANTS AND ESTABLISHED THE NEW AND EVERLASTING COVENANT, THE EUCHARIST! HIS BODY AND BLOOD WERE SACRIFICED ON THE CROSS FOR THE SINS OF ALL AND ARE MADE PRESENT IN THE HOLY EUCHARIST!

ST. IGNATIUS OF ANTIOCH, A FOLLOWER OF ST. JOHN, ALSO TEACHES US ABOUT THE EUCHARIST.

ST. IGNATIUS SAID,

THE EUCHARIST IS THE MEDICINE OF IMMORTALITY AND THE ANTIDOTE AGAINST DEATH, ENABLING US TO LIVE FOREVER IN JESUS CHRIST.

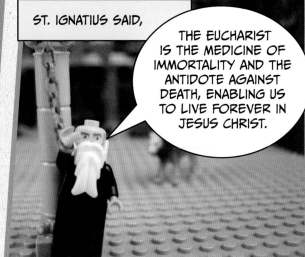

ST. IGNATIUS OF ANTIOCH, PRAY FOR US!

WE WERE BITTEN BY THE VENOM OF SIN IN THE GARDEN OF EDEN, SO WE NEED AN ANTI-VENOM.

ANTI-VENOM IS MADE FROM THE SAME POISON OF THE SNAKE THAT BIT YOU,

BUT IT IS TRANSFORMED AND GIVEN TO YOU AS MEDICINE.

THAT'S WHAT JESUS DID FOR US!

48

HE TOOK THE VENOM, WHICH IS OUR SIN, UPON HIMSELF.

HE DIED ON THE CROSS TO DESTROY SIN!

THEN HE RESURRECTED FROM THE DEAD TO GIVE US HIS FLESH TO CURE US FROM THE ETERNAL DEATH OF SIN.

THE MOST HOLY EUCHARIST IS HIS FLESH, "THE MEDICINE OF IMMORTALITY," "THE ANTI-VENOM," "THE NEW AND EVERLASTING COVENANT," "THE BLESSED SACRAMENT," "THE CUP OF BLESSING!"

1 JN 2:2, RM 4:25, 1 COR 15:21, 1 COR 10:16

REMEMBER, THE CUP OF BLESSING IS THE THIRD CUP OF THE PASSOVER MEAL, WHEN YOU EAT THE LAMB AND THE UNLEAVENED BREAD.

ST. PAUL SAID,

THIS CUP OF BLESSING IS A PARTICIPATION IN THE BODY AND BLOOD OF OUR LORD JESUS CHRIST.

JESUS IS "THE LAMB OF GOD," "THE BREAD OF LIFE," AND "THE CUP OF BLESSING," WHICH WE RECEIVE IN THE EUCHARIST.

50

IN THE GOSPEL OF JOHN, CHAPTER 6, JESUS PERFORMS ANOTHER MIRACLE: THE MULTIPLICATION OF THE LOAVES AND FISH.

THE GOSPEL SAYS THAT IT WAS NEARING THE FEAST OF THE JEWISH PASSOVER.

AMAZING, IT ALWAYS SEEMS TO REFERENCE BACK TO THE PASSOVER!

JESUS TOOK FIVE LOAVES AND TWO FISH, GAVE THANKS, AND DISTRIBUTED THEM TO THE CROWD.

THERE WAS ENOUGH FOR THE CROWD OF 5,000 MEN, NOT INCLUDING WOMEN AND CHILDREN, PLUS 12 BASKETS FILLED WITH LEFTOVERS!

MOSES AND HIS PEOPLE ATE MANNA IN THE WILDERNESS. MANNA IS THE BREAD COME DOWN FROM HEAVEN.

GOD GAVE THEM THIS BREAD FROM HEAVEN TO SUSTAIN THEM ON THEIR JOURNEY IN THE DESERT.

JN 6:1-33

JESUS NOW TELLS US THAT HE IS THE MANNA AND WE MUST EAT OF HIM!

HE IS THE "BREAD OF LIFE."

JESUS SAID, "YOUR ANCESTORS ATE THE MANNA, BUT THEY DIED."

"I AM THE LIVING BREAD. WHOEVER EATS OF ME WILL LIVE FOREVER. I WILL GIVE MY FLESH FOR THE LIFE OF THE WORLD."

JESUS WAS BORN IN BETHLEHEM, A TOWN WHOSE NAME MEANS "HOUSE OF BREAD" AND "HOUSE OF FLESH."

HE WAS WRAPPED IN SWADDLING CLOTHES, WHICH IS WHAT A LAMB BEING SACRIFICED WOULD WEAR.

HE WAS LAID IN A MANGER, WHICH IS WHERE THE SHEEP COME TO EAT.

IMAGINE THAT! JESUS IS THE "BREAD OF LIFE" BORN IN THE "HOUSE OF BREAD." HE IS THE "WORD BECOME FLESH" BORN IN THE "HOUSE OF FLESH." HE IS THE "GOOD SHEPHERD" LAID IN A MANGER WHERE THE SHEEP COME TO EAT! AND HE TELLS US (HIS SHEEP) TO EAT HIS FLESH AND DRINK HIS BLOOD TO HAVE ETERNAL LIFE!

MAT 2:1, LK 2:12, JN 10:11

AFTER JESUS RESURRECTED FROM THE DEAD, HE WALKED SEVEN MILES TO EMMAUS WITH TWO OF HIS FOLLOWERS. BUT THEY DID NOT RECOGNIZE HIM UNTIL ...

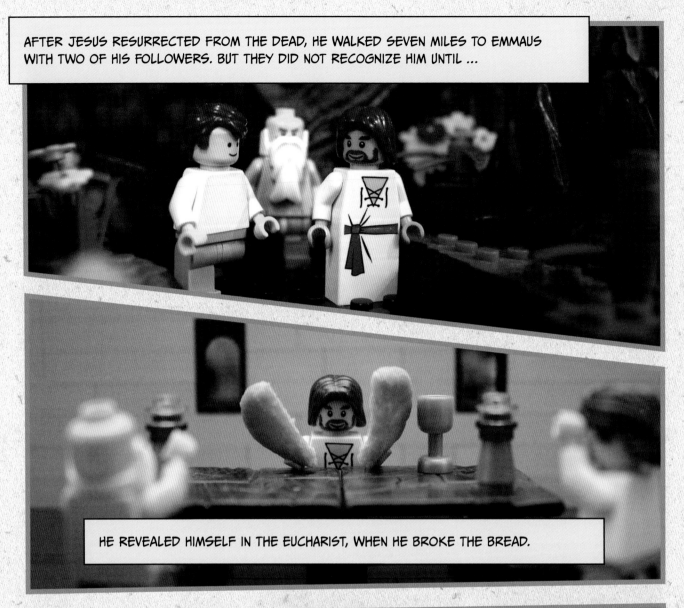

HE REVEALED HIMSELF IN THE EUCHARIST, WHEN HE BROKE THE BREAD.

THE FOLLOWERS OF JESUS FELT THEIR HEARTS WERE ON FIRE WHEN JESUS TOLD THEM ABOUT THE PROPHETS AND THE SCRIPTURE.

IN THE BOOK OF REVELATION, JESUS SAYS,

I STAND AT THE DOOR AND KNOCK TO EAT WITH YOU.

THE BOOK OF REVELATION TEACHES US THAT JESUS WILL GIVE THE HIDDEN MANNA TO THE ONE WHO OVERCOMES (THE ONE WHO TURNS AWAY FROM SIN AND CHOOSES TO DO GOD'S WILL).

JESUS TOLD US THAT HE IS "THE MANNA COME DOWN FROM HEAVEN." HE IS HIDDEN IN THE EUCHARIST.

THE CATHOLIC CHURCH IS "THE BRIDE OF CHRIST" BECAUSE SHE SHARES THE ONE-FLESH, LIFE-GIVING UNION WITH CHRIST.

THE EUCHARIST IS THE TRUE FLESH OF JESUS, AND HE WANTS TO BE UNITED WITH US WHEN WE RECEIVE HIM IN HOLY COMMUNION.

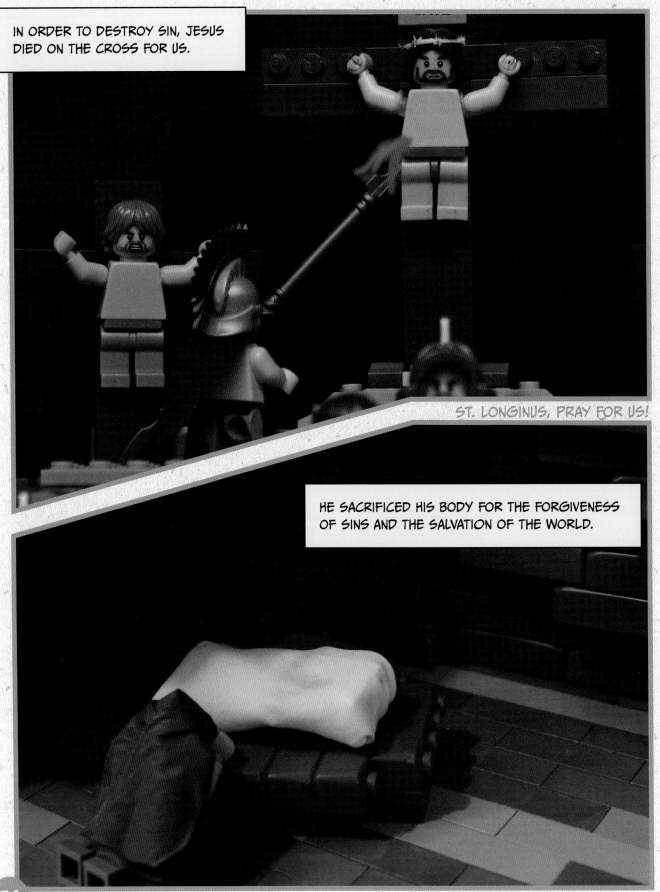

IN ORDER TO DESTROY SIN, JESUS DIED ON THE CROSS FOR US.

ST. LONGINUS, PRAY FOR US!

HE SACRIFICED HIS BODY FOR THE FORGIVENESS OF SINS AND THE SALVATION OF THE WORLD.

WHEN THE PRIEST SAYS THE WORDS OF CONSECRATION, THE BREAD AND WINE TRANSUBSTANTIATE (CHANGE SUBSTANCE). BECAUSE GOD IS OUTSIDE OF TIME, THE SACRIFICE ON THE CROSS IS MADE PRESENT ON THE ALTAR. THE BREAD AND WINE ARE NO LONGER BREAD AND WINE, BUT INSTEAD THEY TRULY BECOME JESUS CHRIST'S BODY, BLOOD, SOUL, AND DIVINITY!

LK 22:19, MAT 26:26, 1 COR 11:24

WE SHOULD ALWAYS BE IN CONSTANT PRAYER DURING THE HOLY MASS AND NOT ALLOW OURSELVES TO BE DISTRACTED.

MOST IMPORTANTLY, WE SHOULD ALWAYS BE IN THE STATE OF GRACE (FREE FROM MORTAL SIN) BEFORE RECEIVING JESUS IN THE HOLY EUCHARIST!

ST. JOHN BOSCO SAID, "YOU CAN FLY TO HEAVEN ON THE WINGS OF CONFESSION AND COMMUNION."

SIMILAR TO THE PASSOVER, THE MASS HAS FOUR TYPES OF PRAYER. FIRST, WE **PRAISE** GOD. THEN, WE OFFER HIM OUR **PETITIONS**. NEXT, WE ASK FOR THE **INTERCESSION** OF THE ANGELS AND SAINTS. FINALLY, WE GIVE **THANKSGIVING** TO GOD FOR HIS SACRIFICE AND HIS MERCY.

AFTER MASS, JESUS IS RESERVED IN THE TABERNACLE (DWELLING PLACE). WHEN WE RECEIVE COMMUNION, WE ALSO BECOME A TABERNACLE OF THE LORD. A SANCTUARY LAMP (RED CANDLE) IS LIT WHEN JESUS IS PRESENT. WE ALL GENUFLECT WHEN WE ENTER OR LEAVE THE CHURCH. IN DOING ALL OF THESE THINGS, WE ARE PROFESSING THAT THE KING OF HEAVEN AND EARTH IS PRESENT!

ROMANS 14:11

WE CAN ALSO ADORE THE LORD WHEN HE IS EXPOSED IN THE MONSTRANCE. THIS IS CALLED ADORATION. DURING THIS TIME, JESUS IS FULLY PRESENT IN THE CONSECRATED HOST INSIDE THE MONSTRANCE. YOU CAN KNEEL OR SIT AND PRAY OR TALK TO GOD IN SILENCE. REMEMBER IN THE GARDEN OF GETHSEMANE WHEN JESUS ASKS HIS APOSTLES, "COULD YOU NOT WAIT ONE HOUR WITH ME?" WELL, THE INVITATION IS THE SAME FOR US NOW. JESUS WANTS US TO WAIT AND PRAY BEFORE HIM IN ADORATION.

JESUS IS TRULY PRESENT, BODY, BLOOD, SOUL, AND DIVINITY. THIS IS WHY WE GENUFLECT (KNEEL) WHEN WE ENTER OR LEAVE THE PEWS.

THE BIBLE SAYS, "EVERY KNEE SHALL BEND AND EVERY TONGUE CONFESS THAT JESUS CHRIST IS LORD." THIS IS WHY WE GENUFLECT, BOW, OR KNEEL WHEN WE RECEIVE COMMUNION. WE ARE RECEIVING THE KING OF HEAVEN AND EARTH!

I AM IN AWE OVER EVERYTHING THAT I JUST LEARNED ABOUT THE EUCHARIST! I CANNOT WAIT TO GO TO HOLY MASS TO RECEIVE JESUS IN THE EUCHARIST!

THE HOLY EUCHARIST IS THE SOURCE AND SUMMIT OF OUR FAITH.

I ALSO KNOW THAT, AS CATHOLICS, WE HAVE A GREAT DEVOTION TO JESUS' MOTHER, MARY. COULD YOU TELL ME MORE ABOUT WHY WE DO?

NOW THAT YOU UNDERSTAND THE EUCHARIST IS THE NEW AND EVERLASTING COVENANT, IT WILL BE EASY FOR YOU TO UNDERSTAND MARY BECAUSE SHE IS THE ARK OF THE NEW COVENANT.

SHE IS THE ARK OF SALVATION BECAUSE SHE CARRIED JESUS IN HER WOMB.

HOW IS SHE AN ARK?

THE ARK (MARY) AND THE COVENANT (JESUS) ARE INSEPARABLE, AS JESUS TOOK ON HIS FLESH THROUGH HIS MOTHER, MARY.

IT ALL GOES BACK TO THE GARDEN OF EDEN.

REMEMBER WHEN ADAM AND EVE SINNED? WELL, THE DEVIL THOUGHT HE HAD OUTSMARTED GOD.

HE THOUGHT ALL OF HUMANITY, WHICH WAS MADE IN GOD'S IMAGE AND LIKENESS, WOULD NOW BE SEPARATED FROM GOD FOREVER!

BUT GOD ALREADY HAD A PLAN TO SAVE HIS PEOPLE!

GOD TOLD THE DEVIL HIS PLAN TO DESTROY SIN.

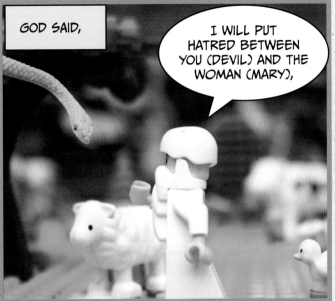

GOD SAID,

I WILL PUT HATRED BETWEEN YOU (DEVIL) AND THE WOMAN (MARY),

BETWEEN HER OFFSPRING (MARY'S) AND YOURS (DEVIL'S).

"SHE (MARY) WILL CRUSH YOUR (DEVIL'S) HEAD."

AND SO IT BEGAN. A NEW PLAN FOR SALVATION, BROUGHT FORTH THROUGH MARY AND JESUS.

GN 3:15

IN THE OLD TESTAMENT, THE OLD ARK WAS MADE TO CARRY THE COVENANT OF GOD. IT WAS MADE SPECIAL AND PURE.

ALTHOUGH IT WAS MADE BY HUMAN HANDS, GOD GAVE THEM SPECIFIC BUILDING INSTRUCTIONS SO THE ARK WOULD BE PERFECT.

THE NEW ARK, MARY, ALSO WAS MADE PERFECTLY PURE (FULL OF GRACE AND SINLESS). SHE CARRIED THE NEW COVENANT (JESUS). YET, UNLIKE THE OLD ARK, WHICH WAS MADE BY HUMAN HANDS, MARY WAS MADE PERFECT BY GOD!

ST. BERNADETTE OF LOURDES, PRAY FOR US!

THE SIMILARITIES BETWEEN THE OLD ARK AND THE NEW ARK ARE NUMEROUS.

JUST LISTEN TO THIS!

MARY WAS OVERSHADOWED BY GOD.

THE ARK WAS THE DWELLING PLACE FOR THE LORD.

JESUS DWELLED WITHIN MARY'S WOMB, AND THE HOLY SPIRIT DWELLED WITHIN HER SOUL.

EX. 40:34, LK 1:46-47

THE OLD ARK CONTAINED THE TEN COMMANDMENTS (THE WORD OF GOD), THE ROD OF AARON (THE HIGH PRIESTHOOD), AND THE MANNA (BREAD FROM HEAVEN).

MARY, THE NEW ARK, CONTAINED JESUS! JESUS IS THE WORD BECOME FLESH, THE HIGH PRIEST, AND THE BREAD FROM HEAVEN.

THE OLD ARK TRAVELED TO THE HILL COUNTRY OF JUDEA.

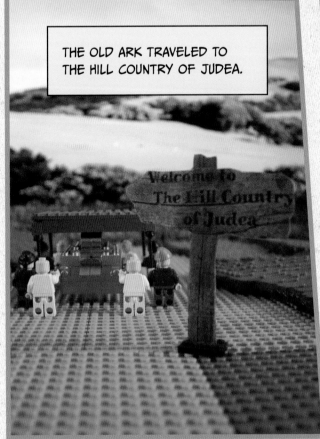

MARY TRAVELED TO THE HILL COUNTRY OF JUDEA.

HEB 9:4, LK 1:42, 2 SM 6:12, LK 1:39

DAVID LEAPT FOR JOY IN THE PRESENCE OF THE ARK.

JOHN THE BAPTIST (INSIDE ELIZABETH'S WOMB) LEAPT FOR JOY IN THE PRESENCE OF THE NEW ARK (MARY).

ST. ELIZABETH, PRAY FOR US!

DAVID SAID, "WHO AM I THAT THE ARK OF MY LORD SHOULD COME TO ME?"

ELIZABETH SAID, "WHO AM I THAT THE MOTHER OF MY LORD SHOULD COME TO ME?"

2 SAM 6:14, LK 1:41, 2 SAM 6:9, LK 1:43

THE OLD ARK STAYED WITH DAVID FOR ABOUT THREE MONTHS.

MARY STAYED WITH HER COUSIN, ELIZABETH, FOR ABOUT THREE MONTHS.

THE OLD ARK RETURNED TO JERUSALEM FOR GOD'S GLORY TO BE REVEALED.

MARY AND JESUS RETURNED TO JERUSALEM FOR GOD'S GLORY TO BE REVEALED.

2 SAM 6:11, LK 1:56, 2 SAM 6:12, LK 2:42-43

WHEN THE GOLDEN ARK LEFT THE TENT OF WORSHIP, IT WAS COVERED WITH A BLUE VEIL.

WHEN MARY APPEARS, SHE IS OFTEN COVERED WITH GOLD AND BLUE.

THE ARK WAS HONORED AND LOVED AMONG JEWS.

MARY IS HONORED AND LOVED AMONG CATHOLICS.

NUM 4:5-6, CCC 839-840, 1 KINGS 3:15, LK 1:48

EXACTLY! IN THE BOOK OF REVELATION, IT SAYS THAT THE WOMAN (MARY) WILL PROTECT HER OFFSPRING FROM THE DRAGON (THE DEVIL).

JUST AS THE ISRAELITES WERE PROTECTED WHEN THEY WERE LED INTO BATTLE WITH THE ARK AND THE COVENANT,

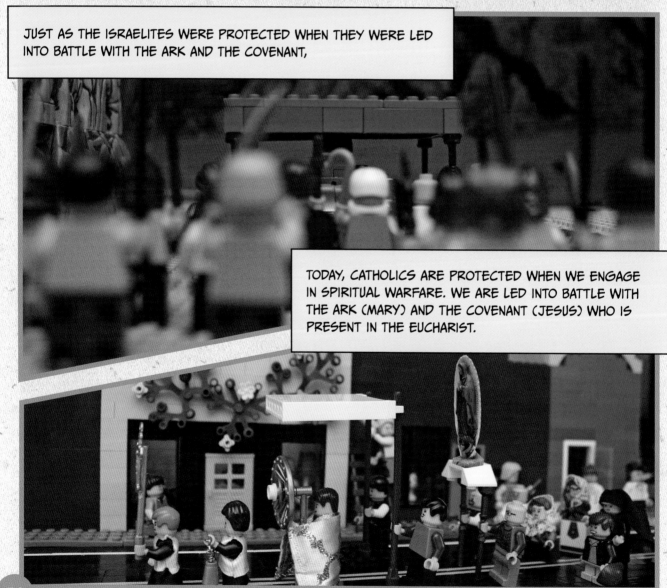

TODAY, CATHOLICS ARE PROTECTED WHEN WE ENGAGE IN SPIRITUAL WARFARE. WE ARE LED INTO BATTLE WITH THE ARK (MARY) AND THE COVENANT (JESUS) WHO IS PRESENT IN THE EUCHARIST.

WOW! MARY REALLY IS THE NEW ARK. THAT'S AMAZING!

SHE IS ALSO THE NEW EVE.

THE NEW EVE? AS IN ADAM AND EVE?

THAT'S RIGHT! EVE TIED THE KNOT OF SIN WHEN THE DEVIL TRICKED HER INTO TAKING THE FRUIT FROM THE FORBIDDEN TREE AND DISOBEYING GOD!

MARY LOOSENED THE KNOT OF SIN WITH HER "FIAT" (YES) TO GOD. SHE OBEYED GOD'S WILL WHEN THE ANGEL GABRIEL TOLD HER GOD'S DIVINE PLAN. MARY SAID,

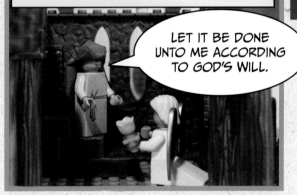

LET IT BE DONE UNTO ME ACCORDING TO GOD'S WILL.

EVE, WHICH MEANS "MOTHER OF THE LIVING," WAS THE FIRST MOTHER OF ALL MANKIND.

MARY, WHO IS JESUS' MOTHER, BECAME THE NEW MOTHER OF ALL MANKIND. JUST BEFORE CHRIST DIED ON THE CROSS, HE GAVE HER TO US THROUGH HIS COMMAND, "BEHOLD YOUR MOTHER."

CCC 975, GEN 3:6, LK 1:38, GEN 3:20, JN 19:26-27

YOU SEE, SIN CAME INTO THE WORLD THE SAME WAY IT LEAVES: GOD WALKS WITH MAN.

THEY ARE IN A GARDEN (THE GARDEN OF EDEN).

A MAN (ADAM) AND A WOMAN (EVE) ARE AT A TREE.

THEY TAKE THE FRUIT FROM THE TREE.

THEY EAT IT.

SIN AND DEATH COME INTO THE WORLD.

AND SIN LEAVES THE WORLD THE SAME WAY IT CAME IN: JESUS (WHO IS GOD) WALKS WITH MAN.

HE IS IN A GARDEN (THE GARDEN OF GETHSEMANE).

A MAN (JESUS) AND A WOMAN (MARY) ARE AT A TREE (THE CROSS).

BUT THIS TIME THE FRUIT (JESUS) IS PUT BACK ON THE TREE (THE CROSS). THIS IS SCRIPTURAL. REMEMBER WHEN ELIZABETH SAID,

BLESSED IS THE **FRUIT** OF YOUR WOMB!

WE MUST EAT OF THE FRUIT OF THAT TREE (THE TREE OF LIFE).

UNLESS YOU EAT MY FLESH AND DRINK MY BLOOD, YOU HAVE NO LIFE IN YOU.

THROUGH THE SACRAMENTS, SIN LEAVES THE WORLD, GOD'S GRACE IS RESTORED IN US, AND WE ARE GIVEN NEW LIFE!

JN 1:14, MAT 26:36, JN 19:25, LK 1:42, JN 6:53, CCC 1129

JUST AS ORIGINAL SIN CAUSED US ALL TO LOSE GRACE AND BE SEPARATED FROM GOD,

GEN 3:23

ADAM AND EVE ATE THE FRUIT AND DIED. NOW WE MUST EAT THE FRUIT IN ORDER TO LIVE. THAT "FRUIT" IS JESUS!

HE IS THE FRUIT OF THE TREE OF LIFE MENTIONED IN THE BOOK OF REVELATION. HE IS THE NEW COVENANT. HE IS THE EUCHARIST!

BY EATING THE FRUIT OF THIS TREE, WE CAN CONQUER DEATH AND HAVE ETERNAL LIFE IN HEAVEN!

MARY IS SO EXTRAORDINARY BECAUSE SHE WAS CHOSEN TO BE THE MOTHER OF JESUS!

SHE IS THE NEW ARK, THE NEW EVE, THE MOTHER OF GOD, THE MOTHER OF THE EUCHARIST, AND THE MOTHER OF THE LIVING.

WOW, FULTON! MARY TRULY IS EXTRAORDINARY!

SHE SURE IS! SHE INTERCEDES FOR US, TOO!

WHAT DO YOU MEAN "INTERCEDES?"

INTERCEDES MEANS THAT MOTHER MARY CAN ASK GOD FOR US ON OUR BEHALF.

DO YOU REMEMBER JESUS' FIRST MIRACLE?

YES, HE TURNED THE WATER INTO WINE AT THE WEDDING FEAST AT CANA.

YES, AND GUESS WHAT TIME OF THE YEAR IT WAS.

PASSOVER?

BINGO!

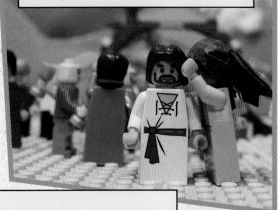

WELL, MARY INTERCEDED FOR THE WEDDING PARTY. SHE ASKED JESUS TO HELP THEM.

JESUS PROVIDED FOR THEM AND BLESSED THEM BECAUSE MARY INTERCEDED ON THEIR BEHALF. THAT WEDDING PARTY SYMBOLIZES US, THE CHURCH. WE CAN ASK MOTHER MARY TO INTERCEDE FOR US WHEN WE PRAY.

CCC 969, JN 2:1-11, JN 2:12, JN 2:3, JN 2:7-11

WE KNOW THAT JESUS KEPT THE TEN COMMANDMENTS PERFECTLY. ONE OF THE COMMANDMENTS IS TO HONOR YOUR FATHER AND MOTHER.

WE, TOO, HONOR MARY BECAUSE WE ARE TO BE LIKE JESUS.

IN THE GOSPEL OF LUKE, MARY TELLS US ALL GENERATIONS WILL CALL HER BLESSED.

WE FULFILL THESE WORDS EVERY TIME WE PRAY THE "HAIL MARY."

ST. LUKE, PRAY FOR US!

HAIL MARY, FULL OF GRACE,
THE LORD IS WITH THEE;
BLESSED ART THOU AMONGST WOMEN,
AND BLESSED IS THE FRUIT OF THY WOMB, JESUS.
HOLY MARY, MOTHER OF GOD, PRAY FOR US SINNERS,
NOW AND AT THE HOUR OF OUR DEATH.
AMEN.

PHIL 2:8, CCC 971, LK 1:48, JN 1:14

THE GREETING OF THE ANGEL GABRIEL:

HAIL MARY, FULL OF GRACE. THE LORD IS WITH YOU.

THE GREETING OF ELIZABETH:

BLESSED ARE YOU AMONG WOMEN AND BLESSED IS THE FRUIT OF YOUR WOMB, JESUS.

AND THE INTERCESSION FOR US, LIKE THAT AT THE WEDDING AT CANA: "HOLY MARY, MOTHER OF GOD, PRAY FOR US SINNERS, NOW AND AT THE HOUR OF OUR DEATH."

WOW, THAT PRAYER IS LOADED!

MARY IS ALSO THE "QUEEN MOTHER."

QUEEN MOTHER?

WHAT IS THAT?

WELL, IN THE OLD TESTAMENT, THE QUEEN MOTHER WAS ALWAYS THE MOTHER OF THE KING JUST AS MARY IS THE MOTHER OF JESUS.

LK 1:28, LK 1:42, JN 2:3, CCC 966, 1 KGS 2:19

MARY WAS ASSUMED INTO HEAVEN AND CROWNED QUEEN OF HEAVEN AND EARTH BY HER SON, JESUS, WHO IS THE KING OF HEAVEN AND EARTH. THAT'S WHY WE CALL HER OUR HEAVENLY MOTHER.

WOW, I NEVER KNEW HOW EXTRAORDINARY MOTHER MARY IS!

I'M GOING TO START ASKING FOR HER INTERCESSION EVERY DAY!

A GREAT WAY TO DO THIS IS TO PRAY THE ROSARY EVERY DAY.

THE ROSARY?

THE ROSARY IS A PRAYER WE PRAY THAT HELPS US MEDITATE ON THE MYSTERIES OF THE LIFE OF JESUS AND PRAY FOR MARY'S INTERCESSION IN OUR LIFE.

CCC 966, CCC 971

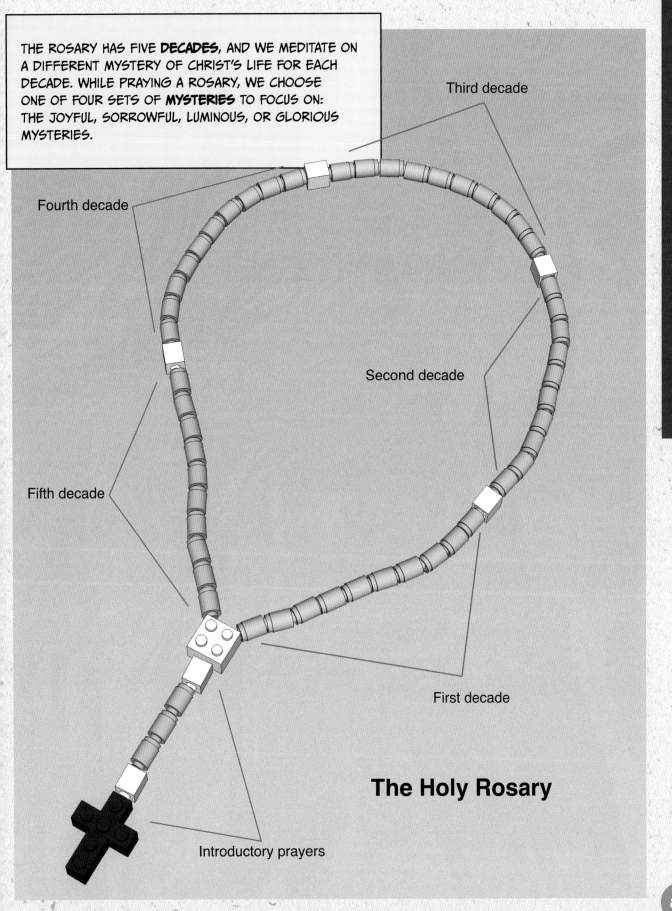

THE ROSARY HAS FIVE **DECADES**, AND WE MEDITATE ON A DIFFERENT MYSTERY OF CHRIST'S LIFE FOR EACH DECADE. WHILE PRAYING A ROSARY, WE CHOOSE ONE OF FOUR SETS OF **MYSTERIES** TO FOCUS ON: THE JOYFUL, SORROWFUL, LUMINOUS, OR GLORIOUS MYSTERIES.

Third decade

Fourth decade

Second decade

Fifth decade

First decade

The Holy Rosary

Introductory prayers

THE **JOYFUL MYSTERIES** CONTEMPLATE THE JOYFUL TIMES IN JESUS' LIFE.

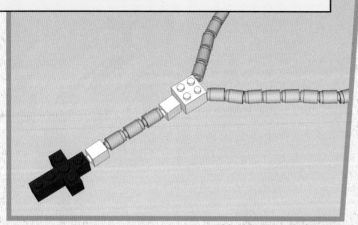

MONDAY AND SATURDAY

THE FIRST JOYFUL MYSTERY IS THE ANNUNCIATION.

THE SECOND JOYFUL MYSTERY IS THE VISITATION.

THE THIRD JOYFUL MYSTERY IS THE NATIVITY.

THE FOURTH JOYFUL MYSTERY IS THE PRESENTATION.

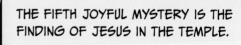

THE FIFTH JOYFUL MYSTERY IS THE FINDING OF JESUS IN THE TEMPLE.

LK 1:26-38, LK 1:39-40, LK 2:1-20, LK 2:22-40, LK 2:49

THE LUMINOUS MYSTERIES
CONTEMPLATE JESUS' PUBLIC LIFE AND MIRACLES.

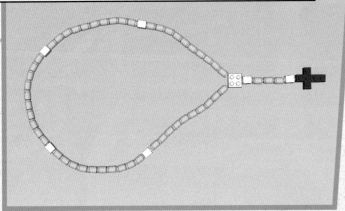

THURSDAY

THE FIRST LUMINOUS MYSTERY IS THE BAPTISM OF THE LORD.

ST. JOHN THE BAPTIST, PRAY FOR US!

THE SECOND LUMINOUS MYSTERY IS THE WEDDING AT CANA.

THE THIRD LUMINOUS MYSTERY IS THE PROCLAMATION OF THE KINGDOM.

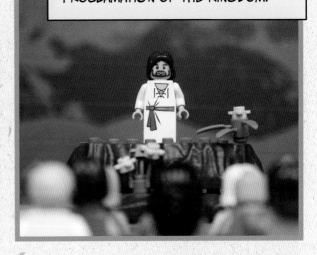

THE FOURTH LUMINOUS MYSTERY IS THE TRANSFIGURATION.

THE FIFTH LUMINOUS MYSTERY IS THE INSTITUTION OF THE EUCHARIST.

MAT 3:13-17, JN 2:1-11, MK 1:14-15, MAT 17:1-3, MK 14:22-24

THE **SORROWFUL MYSTERIES** CONTEMPLATE THE SAD TIMES IN JESUS' LIFE.

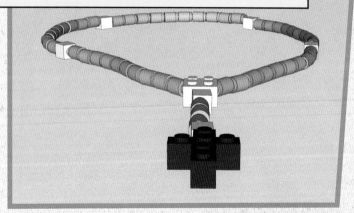

TUESDAY AND FRIDAY

THE FIRST SORROWFUL MYSTERY IS THE AGONY IN THE GARDEN.

THE SECOND SORROWFUL MYSTERY IS THE SCOURGING AT THE PILLAR.

THE THIRD SORROWFUL MYSTERY IS THE CROWNING WITH THORNS.

THE FOURTH SORROWFUL MYSTERY IS THE CARRYING OF THE CROSS.

THE FIFTH SORROWFUL MYSTERY IS THE CRUCIFIXION.

MAT 26:36-46, JN 19:1, JN 19:2, JN 19:17, JN 19:18

THE **GLORIOUS MYSTERIES**
CONTEMPLATE THE PLAN OF SALVATION.

THE FIRST GLORIOUS MYSTERY
IS THE RESURRECTION.

WEDNESDAY AND SUNDAY

THE SECOND GLORIOUS MYSTERY
IS THE ASCENSION.

THE THIRD GLORIOUS MYSTERY IS
THE DESCENT OF THE HOLY SPIRIT.

THE FOURTH GLORIOUS MYSTERY
IS THE ASSUMPTION.

THE FIFTH GLORIOUS MYSTERY
IS THE CORONATION.

MAT 28:5-6, ACTS 1:9, ACTS 2:1-4, CCC 966, REV 12:1

91

1

Sign of the Cross: In the name of the Father, and of the Son, and of the Holy Spirit. Amen.

Apostles' Creed: I believe in God, the Father Almighty, Creator of Heaven and earth. I believe in Jesus Christ, His only Son, our Lord. He was conceived by the power of the Holy Spirit and born of the Virgin Mary. He suffered under Pontius Pilate, was crucified, died, and was buried. He descended into hell. On the third day He rose again. He ascended into Heaven and is seated at the right hand of the Father. He will come again to judge the living and the dead. I believe in the Holy Spirit, the holy Catholic Church, the communion of saints, the forgiveness of sins, the resurrection of the body, and the life everlasting. Amen.

2

Our Father who art in Heaven, hallowed be Thy Name; Thy Kingdom come; Thy will be done on earth as it is in Heaven. Give us this day our daily bread, and forgive us our trespasses, as we forgive those who trespass against us, and lead us not into temptation, but deliver us from evil. Amen.

3

Hail Mary, full of grace, the Lord is with thee. Blessed art thou amongst women, and blessed is the fruit of thy womb, Jesus. Holy Mary, Mother of God, pray for us sinners, now and at the hour of our death. Amen.

4

Glory be to the Father, and to the Son, and to the Holy Spirit, as it was in the beginning, is now, and ever shall be, world without end. Amen.

5

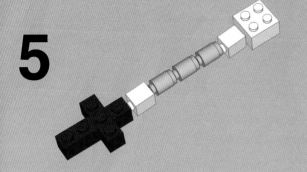

6

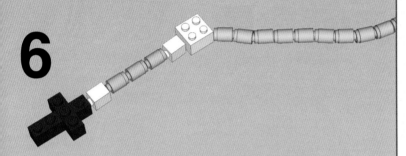

7

Fatima Prayer: O my Jesus, forgive us our sins, save us from the fires of hell, and lead all souls to Heaven, especially those in most need of Thy mercy.

8

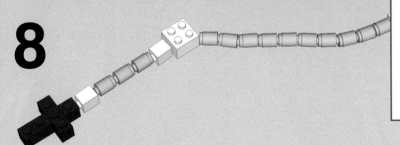

ROSARY INSTRUCTIONS

Start by choosing which set of mysteries you will meditate on. Suggestions: Joyful on Monday & Saturday, Luminous on Thursday, Sorrowful on Tuesday & Friday, Glorious on Wednesday & Sunday.

1. Begin with the Sign of the Cross, followed by the Apostles' Creed prayer.

2. Pray one Our Father prayer, also called The Lord's Prayer.

3. Pray three Hail Mary prayers for the virtues of faith, hope, and charity.

4. Pray one Glory Be prayer.

5. State the first mystery, and pray one Our Father prayer.

6. Pray 10 Hail Mary prayers while contemplating the stated mystery.

7. Conclude the decade by praying the Glory Be prayer and the Fatima Prayer.

8. Continue saying four more decades, meditating on each of the five mysteries in order.

9. Conclude the decades by praying the Hail Holy Queen prayer.

10. Some people also recite the Rosary Prayer, the *Memorare*, and the Prayer to St. Michael the Archangel. Some also recite one Our Father prayer, one Hail Mary prayer, and one Glory Be prayer for the intentions of the pope.

11. Finally, conclude with the Sign of the Cross.

9

Hail, Holy Queen, mother of mercy, our life, our sweetness, and our hope. To thee do we cry, poor banished children of Eve. To thee do we send up our sighs, mourning and weeping in this valley of tears. Turn then, most gracious advocate, thine eyes of mercy toward us, and after this our exile show us the blessed fruit of thy womb, Jesus. O clement, O loving, O sweet Virgin Mary. Pray for us, O Holy Mother of God. That we may be made worthy of the promises of Christ.

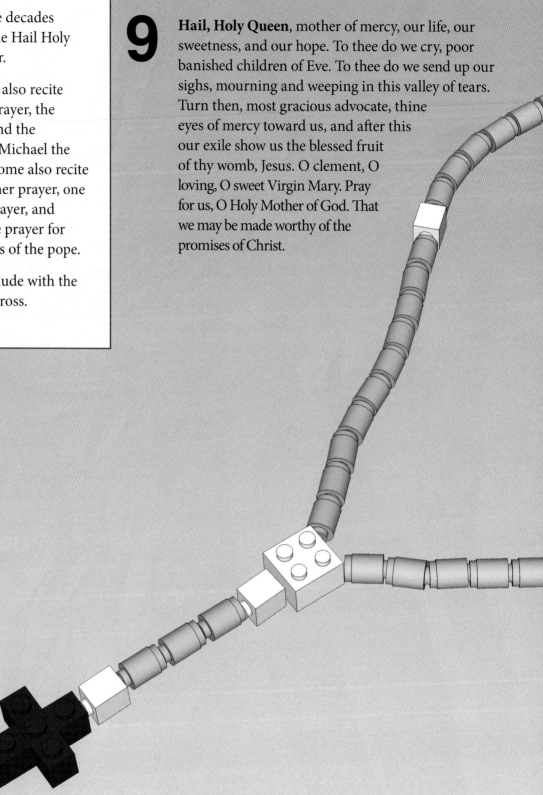

10 **The Rosary Prayer:** Let us pray: O God, whose Only Begotten Son, by His life, death, and resurrection, has purchased for us the rewards of eternal life, grant, we beseech Thee, that while meditating on these mysteries of the most holy Rosary of the Blessed Virgin Mary, we may imitate what they contain and obtain what they promise, through the same Christ our Lord. Amen.

Memorare: Remember, O most gracious Virgin Mary, that never was it known that anyone who fled to thy protection, implored thy help, or sought thine intercession was left unaided. Inspired by this confidence, I fly unto thee, O Virgin of virgins, my mother; to thee do I come, before thee I stand, sinful and sorrowful. O Mother of the Word incarnate, despise not my petitions, but in thy mercy hear and answer me. Amen.

For the Pope's intentions: **Our Father ...**, **Hail Mary ...**, **Glory Be ...**, **Prayer to St. Michael the Archangel:** St. Michael the Archangel, defend us in battle. Be our protection against the wickedness and snares of the devil. May God rebuke him, we humbly pray, and do thou, O Prince of the heavenly host, by the power of God, cast into hell Satan, and all the evil spirits, who prowl about the world seeking the ruin of souls. Amen.

11 **Sign of the Cross:** In the name of the Father, and of the Son, and of the Holy Spirit. Amen.

JN 19:25

BAPTISM

JN 6:53, CCC 1215, TI 3:5, JN 3:5

EXACTLY! IN THE BIBLE, THE WATER AND THE SPIRIT MAKE THINGS NEW.

IN THE BEGINNING WHEN THE WORLD WAS CREATED, IT WAS ALL WATER, AND THE SPIRIT HOVERED ABOVE IT.

THEN GOD CALLED THE GROUND OUT OF THE WATER. IT WAS A NEW CREATION THROUGH THE WATER AND THE SPIRIT.

GEN 1:2, GEN 8:8, EX 14:23-24, MAT 3:16, GEN 1:9-10

MANY YEARS LATER DURING THE TIME OF NOAH, THE WORLD TURNED WICKED, AND GOD, IN HIS MERCY, DECIDED TO MAKE IT NEW.

IT RAINED FOR 40 DAYS AND 40 NIGHTS. GOD USED THE WATER OF THE FLOOD TO CLEANSE HIS CREATION OF EVIL (SIN).

AFTER THE FLOOD, NOAH RELEASED THE DOVE, A SYMBOL OF THE HOLY SPIRIT.

GEN 6: 5–13, GEN 7:12, GEN 8:8–12

GOD'S CREATION WAS RENEWED THROUGH THE WATER AND THE SPIRIT, WHICH PREFIGURED BAPTISM.

MAT 3:16

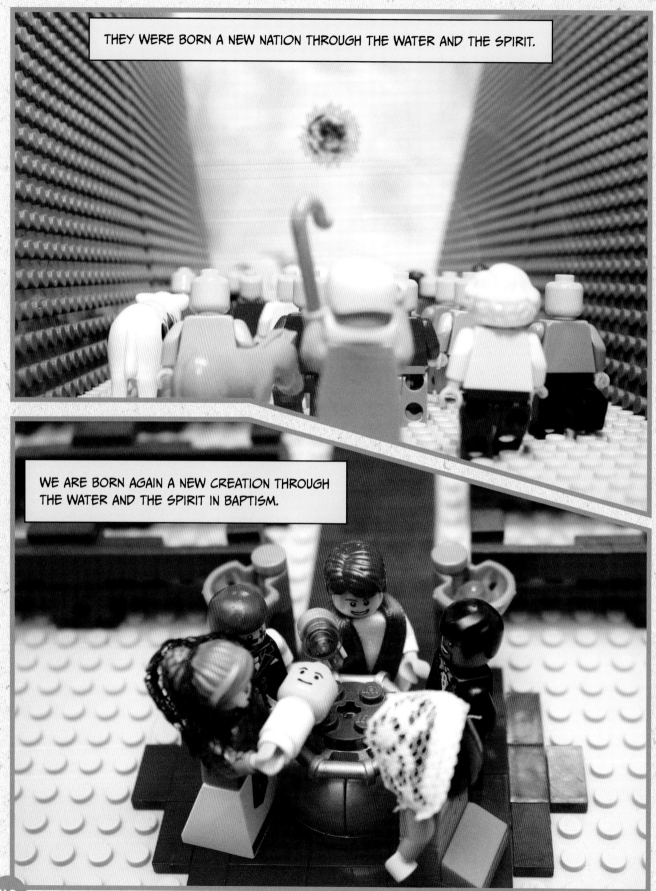

THE ISRAELITES WERE LED INTO BATTLE WITH THE ARK AND THE COVENANT.

WE ARE LED INTO SPIRITUAL BATTLE WITH THE ARK (MARY) AND THE COVENANT (JESUS IN THE EUCHARIST).

THAT'S WHY WE NEED TO BE BAPTIZED! IT'S HOW WE BECOME BORN AGAIN,

NOT INTO THE ORIGINAL SIN OF ADAM AND EVE, BUT AS A NEW CREATION IN CHRIST AND A CHILD OF GOD.

ST. PAUL TELLS US,

WE ARE BAPTIZED INTO THE RESURRECTION OF CHRIST.

ST. PAUL, PRAY FOR US!

CHRIST'S PASSION, DEATH, AND RESURRECTION DEFEATED SIN AND DEATH AND OPENED HEAVEN'S GATES.

THE RESURRECTION IS THE DAY OF NEW CREATION, THE EIGHTH DAY.

WHAT IS THE EIGHTH DAY?

GOD ORIGINALLY CREATED THE WORLD IN SIX DAYS, AND ON THE SEVENTH DAY, SATURDAY, HE RESTED. THAT WAS THE SABBATH DAY (DAY RESERVED TO WORSHIP GOD AND REST).

JN 3:5, RM 6:4-5, REV 1:18, CCC 2174, GEN 1:1-2:4

SO WHILE JEWS OBSERVE THE SABBATH ON SATURDAY,

CHRISTIANS RECOGNIZE THAT THE RESURRECTION OF CHRIST FULFILLS THE SABBATH. WE CELEBRATE THE SABBATH ON SUNDAY.

THIS IS WHY WE GO TO MASS ON SUNDAY NOW. IT'S THE FIRST DAY OF THE WEEK, THE DAY OF THE RESURRECTION, THE DAY OF NEW CREATION, THE EIGHTH DAY!

THAT MAKES SENSE! I'VE ALWAYS WONDERED WHY WE GO TO MASS ON SUNDAYS.

EX 20:8, ACTS 20:7, CCC 2174, ACTS 20:7

THAT'S WHY WHENEVER WE ARE BAPTIZED, WHETHER WE ARE 1 DAY OLD,

OR 90 YEARS OLD,

WE ARE BAPTIZED INTO THE EIGHTH DAY, THE DAY OF THE RESURRECTION!

THE EIGHT SIDES ALSO REMIND US OF THE EIGHT PEOPLE SAVED ON NOAH'S ARK.

THOSE EIGHT PEOPLE WHO WERE SAVED PREFIGURE (REPRESENT) THE EIGHTH DAY, THE DAY OF NEW CREATION AND BAPTISM.

ST. PETER SAYS,

ACTS 2:38, 1 PT 2:5, CCC 901-913

MAT 28:19, CCC 1279, ACTS 2:38, ACTS 2:39

THE ULTIMATE RESPONSIBILITY OF PARENTS IS TO BRING THEIR CHILD INTO THE FAMILY OF GOD THROUGH BAPTISM. THEY MAKE A DECLARATION OF FAITH ON BEHALF OF THE CHILD AND PROMISE TO TEACH THE CHILD TO REJECT SIN AND EMBRACE THE TRUTHS OF THE CATHOLIC FAITH.

IT'S ALSO THEIR RESPONSIBILITY TO RAISE THE CHILD IN THE PRACTICES OF THE CHURCH.

IN THE NAME OF THE FATHER ...

THEY SHOULD TEACH THE CHILD TO OBEY THE TEN COMMANDMENTS BY LOVING GOD AND LOVING NEIGHBORS.

THESE PRACTICES WILL HELP THE CHILD LIVE A LIFE THAT LEADS TO ETERNAL SALVATION!

CCC 1255, CCC 2225-2226, CCC 2083

MAT 28:19, CCC 1279, CCC 1212

Rite of Baptism

1   Proclamation of the Gospel. Hear the Word of God, choose to reject sin, and make promises to live for Christ.

2   *Oleum Sanctorum* (Oil of Catechumens). Anointed by the Holy Spirit, join Christ's mission of priest, prophet, and king.

3   White Garment. Put on Christ and rise with Him.

4   Prayer of Epiclesis. Invoke the Holy Spirit upon the water to be baptized by water and the Spirit.

5   Water. Be cleansed with water, die to sin, and be born into the Trinity.

6   Godparents. Present the child and take co-responsibility for the child's religious education.

7   Candle. Enlightened by Christ, be the light of Christ to the world.

8   Easter Candle. Remember the Paschal Mystery: the Passion, Death, and Resurrection of Jesus.

9   Sign of the cross. Be claimed for Christ through the grace of His cross.

10 Essential Rite. "I baptize you in the name of the Father, and of the Son, and of the Holy Spirit." Pour water three times.

CCC 1234-1243, ACTS 2:38, CCC 1272, RM 8:29

RECONCILIATION

RM 3:23-24, CCC 1486, CCC 1487-1489

NM 14:34, NM 11:1, HEB 11:29, JAS 2:17, EX 32:1-4

CCC 1854-1855, 1 JN 5:16-17

SCRIPTURE SAYS THERE ARE SINS THAT ARE NOT UNTO DEATH (VENIAL)

AND SINS THAT ARE UNTO DEATH (MORTAL).

BANK

1 JN 5:16-17

CCC 1861, CCC 1451-1454, MT 5-7, RM 12-15

A MORTAL SIN HAS THREE CONDITIONS:
1. IT MUST BE A GRAVE ACT: IT MUST BE INTRINSICALLY EVIL AND IMMORAL.
2. YOU MUST HAVE FULL KNOWLEDGE: YOU MUST KNOW THAT IT IS WRONG.
3. YOU MUST HAVE DELIBERATE CONSENT: YOU MUST FREELY CHOOSE TO DO IT.

CCC 1858-1859, MK 10:19, LK 16:19-31

HOME
SWEET HOM
THAT IS GOOD NEWS! I WANT TO SHARE IT. CAN YOU TELL ME MORE ABOUT RECONCILIATION?
OF COURSE!
DID YOU KNOW, IN THE BIBLE, GOD BREATHED ON HIS PEOPLE TWO TIMES?

THE FIRST TIME WAS WHEN GOD BREATHED LIFE INTO THE NOSTRILS OF ADAM.

IT WASN'T LONG AFTER THIS THAT ADAM SINNED AND DEATH CAME INTO THE WORLD.

AFTER ADAM SINNED, GOD ASKED HIM,

WHAT HAVE YOU DONE?

EVEN GOD, WHO KNOWS EVERYTHING, WANTED ADAM TO CONFESS HIS SINS.

GN 3:6, GN 3:11

THE SECOND TIME GOD BREATHED ON HIS PEOPLE WAS AFTER THE RESURRECTION. JESUS, WHO IS GOD, APPEARED TO HIS APOSTLES IN THE UPPER ROOM, AND HE BREATHED ON THEM.

AFTER JESUS BREATHED ON HIS APOSTLES, HE SAID,

WHOSE SINS YOU FORGIVE ARE FORGIVEN THEM, AND WHOSE SINS YOU RETAIN ARE RETAINED.

THE CHURCH AND THE APOSTLES, WHO WERE THE FIRST PRIESTS, WERE GIVEN AUTHORITY FROM AND THROUGH GOD TO FORGIVE SINS.

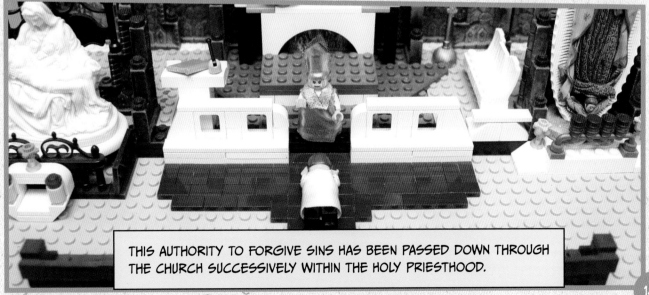

THIS AUTHORITY TO FORGIVE SINS HAS BEEN PASSED DOWN THROUGH THE CHURCH SUCCESSIVELY WITHIN THE HOLY PRIESTHOOD.

JN 20:23, CCC 1461, 2 COR 5:18, CCC 1120, LK 24:47, MT 28:18-20

WE NEED FORGIVENESS OF SINS THROUGH RECONCILIATION BECAUSE IT BREATHES GOD'S LIFE BACK INTO US

AND FILLS US WITH GOD'S GRACE SO WE CAN RECEIVE THE HOLY EUCHARIST!

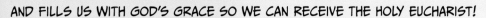

CCC 1997, CCC 1468, LK 15:32

143

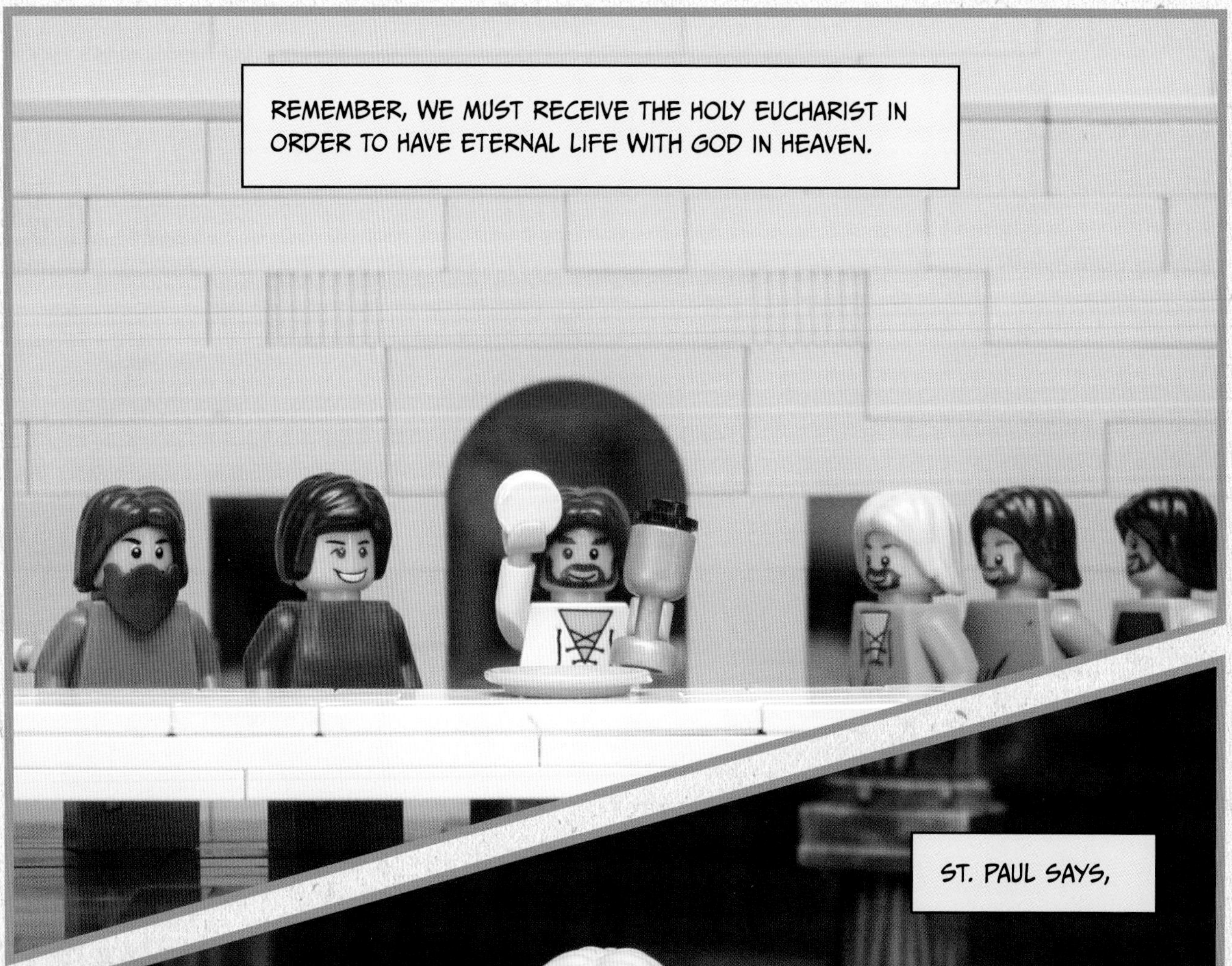

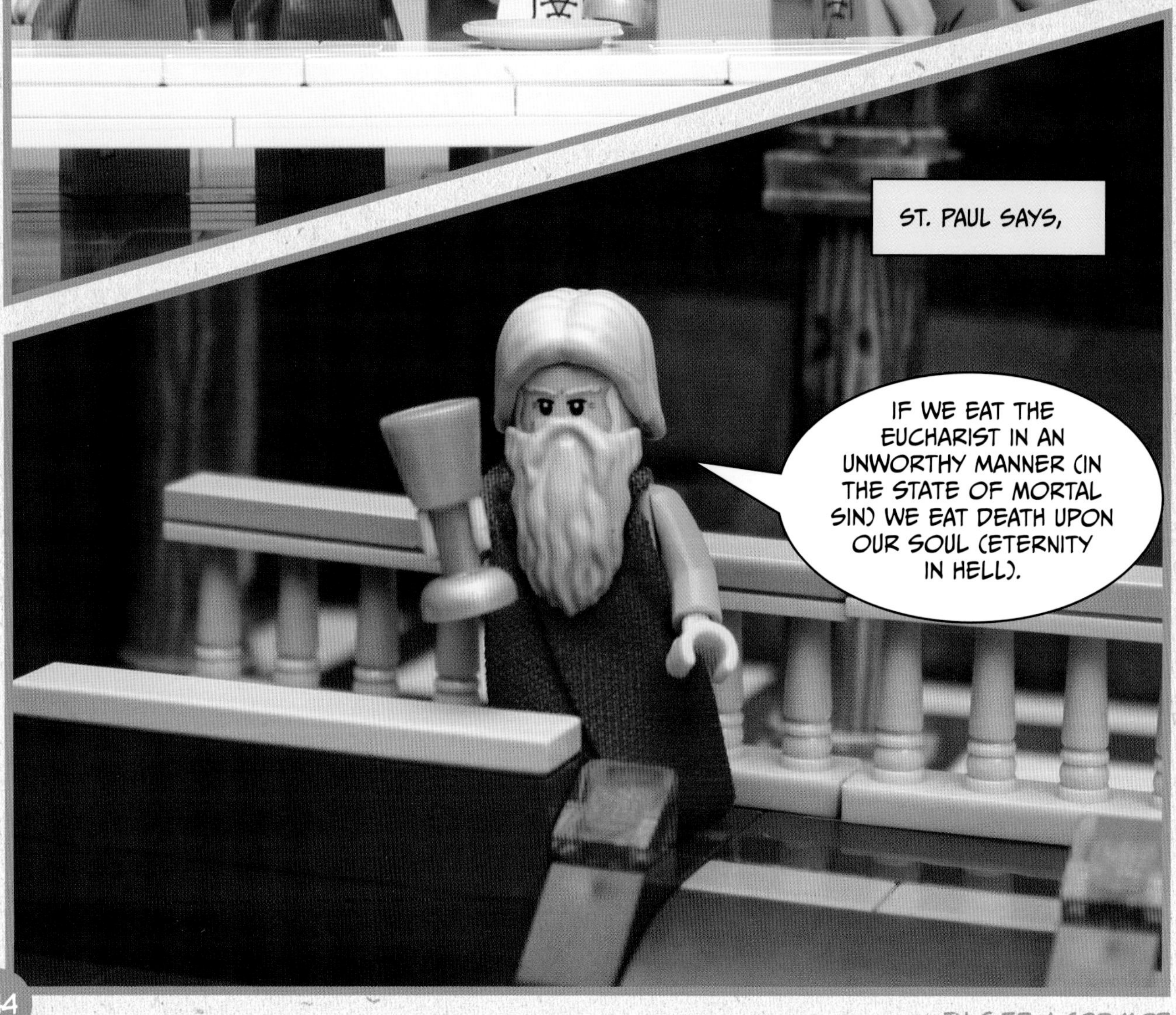

JN 6:53, 1 COR 11:27

JUST THINK OF WHEN GOD SPOKE INTO THE DARKNESS AND CREATED THE LIGHT.

OR WHEN ALL WHO WERE PRESENT IN THE GARDEN OF GETHSEMANE WERE KNOCKED TO THE GROUND WHEN CHRIST SAID,

I AM!

THE EUCHARIST (WHICH IS GOD) IS THE SAME POWER SOURCE THAT CREATED THE UNIVERSE!

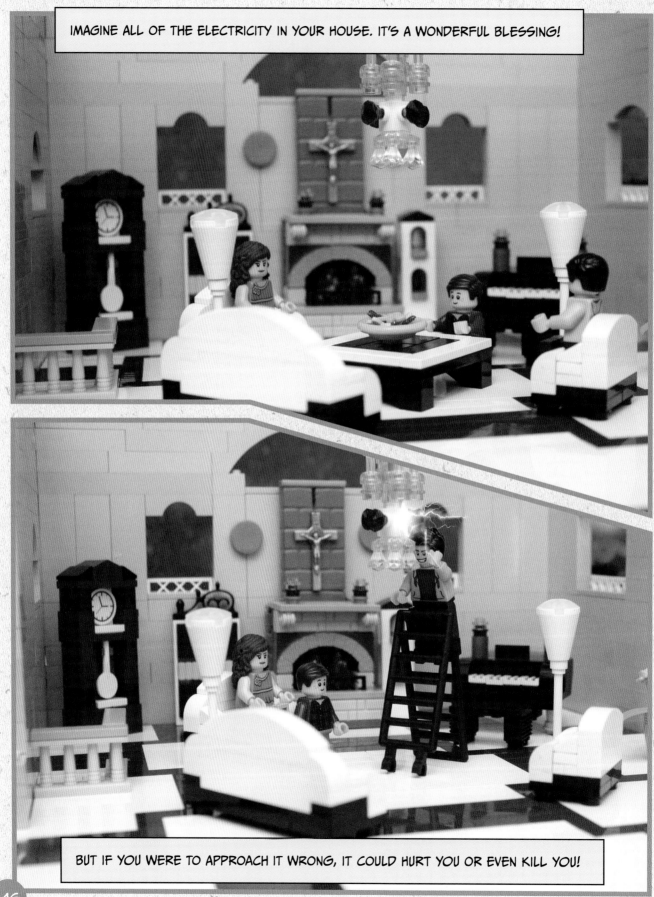

THE EUCHARIST IS GOD ALMIGHTY! IT IS SACRED AND POWERFUL!

IT IS GOD BECOME FLESH UNDER THE FORM OF BREAD AND WINE.

THEREFORE, IT MUST BE APPROACHED CORRECTLY. OUR SOUL MUST BE CLEAN!

ST. JOHN VIANNEY, PRAY FOR US!

YOU WOULDN'T EAT YOUR FOOD AFTER TAKING OUT THE GARBAGE WITHOUT WASHING YOUR HANDS, RIGHT?

THIS COULD MAKE YOU SICK OR EVEN KILL YOU!

147

CCC 1333, CCC 1376, MT 26:26, MK 14:22, LK 22:19, 1 COR 11:24, 1 COR 11:27

THE SAME IS TRUE ABOUT THE EUCHARIST, WHICH IS A FAMILY MEAL.

WE HAVE A LOVING FATHER WHO WAITS AT THE TABLE FOR US,

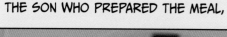

THE SON WHO PREPARED THE MEAL,

THE HOLY SPIRIT WHO UNITES US,

AND A MOTHER WHO CALLS US TO THE SUPPER.

BUT REMEMBER, YOU MUST FIRST "WASH UP" IN THE SACRAMENT OF RECONCILIATION.

1 COR 10:16-17, 1 THES 1:10, CCC 1359, CCC 690, JN 16:14, CCC 964, 1 COR 11:28

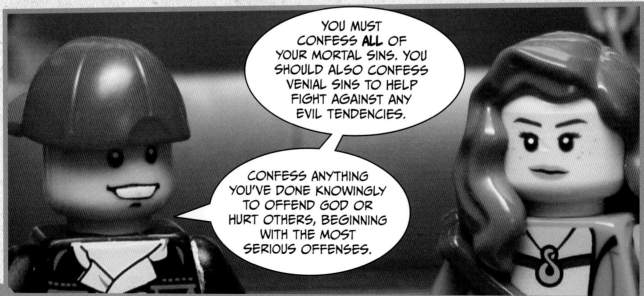

CCC 1455-1458

I SEE HOW IMPORTANT RECONCILIATION IS NOW!

CAN YOU REMIND ME WHAT I SHOULD DO WHEN I GO TO THE SACRAMENT OF RECONCILIATION?

SURE!

FIRST YOU ASK THE HOLY SPIRIT IN PRAYER TO HELP YOU REMEMBER YOUR SINS.

THEN YOU DO AN EXAMINATION OF CONSCIENCE BY CALLING TO MIND YOUR PAST THOUGHTS, WORDS, ACTIONS, AND NEGLECTS. YOU CAN USE THE TEN COMMANDMENTS AS YOUR GUIDE.

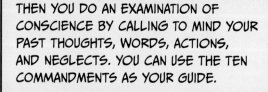

CCC 1453, CCC 1454

THE FIRST THREE CONCERN LOVE OF GOD,

I   I AM THE LORD YOUR GOD. YOU SHALL WORSHIP THE LORD YOUR GOD AND HIM ONLY SHALL YOU SERVE.

II YOU SHALL NOT TAKE THE NAME OF THE LORD YOUR GOD IN VAIN.

III REMEMBER TO KEEP HOLY THE SABBATH DAY.

AND THE OTHER SEVEN CONCERN LOVE OF NEIGHBOR.

IV HONOR YOUR FATHER AND YOUR MOTHER.

V YOU SHALL NOT KILL.

VI YOU SHALL NOT COMMIT ADULTERY.

VII YOU SHALL NOT STEAL

VIII YOU SHALL NOT BEAR FALSE WITNESS AGAINST YOUR NEIGHBOR.

IX YOU SHALL NOT COVET YOUR NEIGHBOR'S WIFE.

X YOU SHALL NOT COVET YOUR NEIGHBOR'S GOODS.

CCC 2067, EX 20:1-17

THE PRIEST MAY THEN TALK TO YOU TO GIVE YOU GUIDANCE ON HOW TO AVOID THESE SINS IN THE FUTURE.

HE WILL GIVE YOU A PENANCE, WHICH IS A WAY FOR YOU TO MAKE AMENDS FOR YOUR SINS. IT'S USUALLY A TASK SUCH AS A FEW PRAYERS TO RECITE OR AN ACT OF KINDNESS TOWARD OTHERS.

HE WILL ASK YOU TO RECITE AN ACT OF CONTRITION LIKE THIS ONE:

Act of Contrition

O my God, I am heartily sorry for having offended Thee, and I detest all my sins, because I dread the loss of Heaven, and the pains of hell; but most of all because they offend Thee, my God, Who are all good and deserving of all my love. I firmly resolve, with the help of Thy grace, to confess my sins, to do penance, and to amend my life. Amen.

CCC 1459-1460

AND YOU NEVER HAVE TO WORRY BECAUSE A PRIEST IS NOT PERMITTED TO TELL ANY OF YOUR SINS TO ANYONE, NO MATTER WHAT! NOT THE POLICE, NOT YOUR PARENTS, NO ONE!

THE BEST PART OF RECEIVING A SACRAMENTAL CONFESSION IS THAT YOU ARE PERFECTLY CLEAN AND FULL OF GRACE AGAIN.

THIS MEANS YOU CAN RECEIVE THE EUCHARIST!

CCC 1467, CCC 1432, MK 1:15, MAT 26:26-28

BAPTISM REMOVES SIN, RESTORES GRACE, AND BRINGS US BACK INTO GOD'S FAMILY.

CCC 1324, CCC 1279

CCC 1496, MAT 26:28, JN 3:16

IF SIN EQUALS DEATH, THEN WHAT EQUALS THE DEATH OF SIN?

WELL, THE BIBLE SAYS BAPTISM REMOVES SIN.

THE BIBLE SAYS CONFESSION REMOVES SIN.

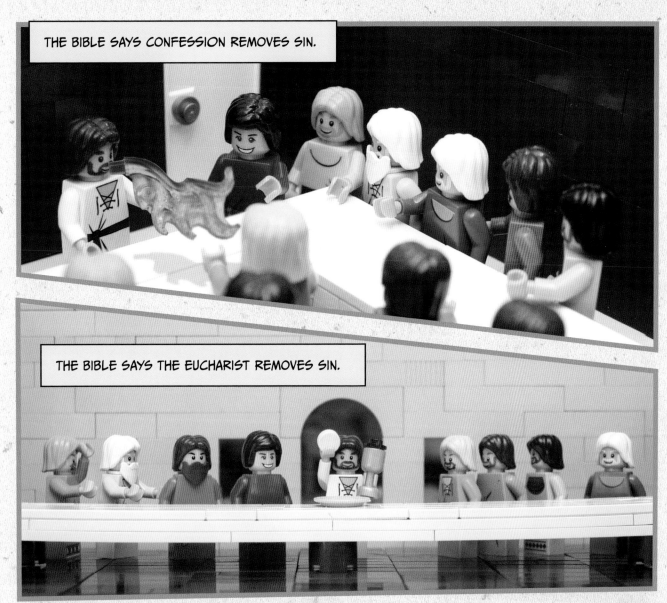

THE BIBLE SAYS THE EUCHARIST REMOVES SIN.

SO, WE CAN CONCLUDE:

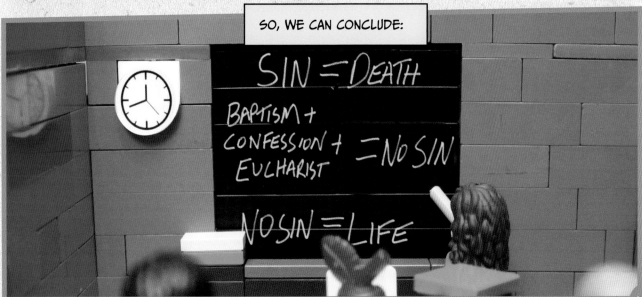

SIN = DEATH

BAPTISM +
CONFESSION + = NO SIN
EUCHARIST

NO SIN = LIFE

CCC 1127, CCC 1113

CONFIRMATION

CCC 2003, CCC 1212, CCC 1285, CCC 1254-1255, CCC 1308

HEB 6:1, CCC 2041-2043

IT IS A LOT OF RESPONSIBILITY, BUT WE CAN CHOOSE A SPONSOR (A CONFIRMED ADULT ROLE MODEL) TO HELP GUIDE US IN OUR CHRISTIAN LIFE.

WE ALSO CHOOSE A SAINT (A PERSON WHO IS IN HEAVEN UNITED WITH GOD) WHO IS A ROLE MODEL FOR HOLINESS AND SOMEONE WE CAN TURN TO FOR INTERCESSION.

ST. GIANNA BERETTA-MOLLA, PRAY FOR US!

THROUGH THE SACRAMENT OF CONFIRMATION, WE RECEIVE GIFTS FROM GOD TO HELP US LIVE AN AUTHENTICALLY CHRISTIAN LIFE. CHRIST PROMISED TO GIVE US HIS GIFTS THROUGH THE HOLY SPIRIT.

CCC 1311, CCC 956, MK 12:27, JN 14:26

AT PENTECOST, WHEN THE HOLY SPIRIT DESCENDED LIKE TONGUES OF FIRE, ALL PRESENT WERE FILLED WITH THE HOLY SPIRIT, WHICH ENABLED THEM TO PROCLAIM THE GOSPEL.

DURING THE RITE OF CONFIRMATION, THE BISHOP LAYS HANDS ON THE CONFIRMANDS AND ANOINTS THEM WITH SACRUM CHRISMA (HOLY CHRISM OIL). THE CONFIRMANDS ARE SEALED WITH THE GIFT OF THE THE HOLY SPIRIT, WHICH GIVES THEM THE GRACES NECESSARY TO PROCLAIM AND LIVE THE GOSPEL.

BE SEALED WITH THE GIFT OF THE HOLY SPIRIT.

ACTS 2:1-11, CCC 1289

WE RECEIVE AN INCREASE IN THE SEVEN GIFTS OF THE HOLY SPIRIT.

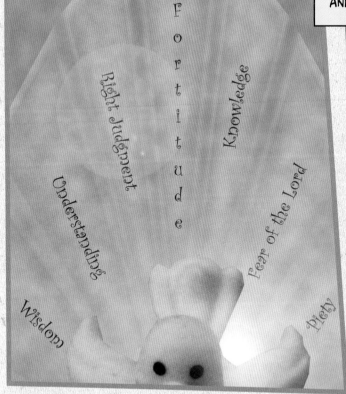

Fortitude

Right Judgment

Knowledge

Understanding

Fear of the Lord

Wisdom

Piety

WISDOM ALLOWS US TO SEE THINGS AS GOD DOES AND TO DESIRE GOD AND NOT THE WORLD.

J.M.J.

If the new crime be, to believe in God, let us all be criminals.

UNTIL NEXT TIME, GOD LOVE YOU!

VEN. ARCHBISHOP FULTON J. SHEEN, PRAY FOR US!

UNDERSTANDING HELPS US TO UNDERSTAND THE FAITH. IT GIVES US INSIGHT THROUGH PRAYER, SCRIPTURE, AND THE SACRAMENTS.

RIGHT JUDGMENT OR COUNSEL HELPS US TO AVOID SIN THROUGH KNOWLEDGE OF RIGHT AND WRONG.

ST. PADRE PIO, PRAY FOR US!

CCC 1303, IS 11:1-2, CCC 1831, CCC 1845

FORTITUDE OR COURAGE ALLOWS US TO ENDURE EVIL, DEFEND OUR FAITH, AND PERSEVERE IN THE LIFE OF CHRIST.

ST. JOAN OF ARC, PRAY FOR US!

KNOWLEDGE IS THE ACTUAL ABILITY TO JUDGE ALL THINGS ACCORDING TO THE TRUTHS OF THE CATHOLIC FAITH AND TO SEE THE CIRCUMSTANCES OF OUR LIFE THE WAY THAT GOD SEES THEM.

ST. THOMAS AQUINAS, PRAY FOR US!

PIETY IS THE WILLINGNESS TO WORSHIP AND OBEY GOD.

ST. TERESA OF CALCUTTA, PRAY FOR US!

FEAR OF THE LORD GIVES US THE DESIRE NOT TO OFFEND GOD OUT OF LOVE FOR HIM.

ST. AUGUSTINE, PRAY FOR US!

CCC 1304, 1317, 2 COR 1:21-22

THE EARLY CHURCH FATHER THEOPHILUS ASKED,

ARE YOU UNWILLING TO BE ANOINTED WITH THE OIL OF GOD?

IT IS ON THIS ACCOUNT THAT WE ARE CALLED CHRISTIANS:

BECAUSE WE ARE ANOINTED.

BECAUSE OUR ANOINTING MARKS US AS SOLDIERS FOR CHRIST, WE MUST NOW STAND UP AND FIGHT FOR OUR FAITH.

THINK ABOUT A SOLDIER'S JOB. IT'S AN INTENSE DUTY!

BUT CHRIST ARMS US WITH HIS GRACE, THE GIFTS OF THE HOLY SPIRIT, AND OUR CHRISTIAN TRAINING. SO, FIGHTING FOR CHRIST IS A SOURCE OF GREAT JOY!

WE ARE NOW ARMED AND READY TO REPRESENT THE KINGDOM OF GOD

AND PROCLAIM OUR FAITH.

THIS IS WHY JESUS SAYS, "BE NOT AFRAID."

BECAUSE IT TAKES COURAGE TO SHARE YOUR FAITH!

ASHES ON OUR FOREHEADS REMIND US AND SHOW OTHERS THAT OUR VERY EXISTENCE IS A GIFT FROM GOD.

THE SIGN OF THE CROSS REMINDS US AND SHOWS OTHERS THAT EVERYTHING WE RECEIVE IS FROM GOD, INCLUDING SALVATION.

IN THE NAME OF THE FATHER ...

CRUCIFIXES, HOLY MEDALS, AND SCAPULARS KEEP US ALL AWARE OF CHRIST'S PRESENCE IN OUR DAILY LIVES.

CCC 1667, CCC 1668, CCC 1672

IT'S IMPORTANT TO VISIBLY FOLLOW CHRIST AND OPENLY SHARE OUR FAITH WITH OTHERS.

JESUS SAID,

IF YOU DENY ME IN FRONT OF OTHERS, I WILL DENY YOU IN FRONT OF MY FATHER.

MAT 4:19, MAT 10:33

SUFFERING IS HOLY TO GOD.

OUR SUFFERING IS A PARTICIPATION IN THE SAME CURRENCY THAT PURCHASED OUR SALVATION.

WE ALSO ARE ASKED TO WORK. THERE ARE TWO TYPES OF WORK WE CAN DO: CORPORAL WORKS (FOR THE BODY) AND SPIRITUAL WORKS (FOR THE SOUL).

1 PT 4:12-19, 1 PT 2:21, GAL 3:13-15, RM 2:6-11

THE SEVEN CORPORAL WORKS OF MERCY ARE:

FEED THE HUNGRY,

GIVE DRINK TO THE THIRSTY,

CLOTHE THE NAKED,

MAT 25:34-40, CCC 2447

SHELTER THE HOMELESS,

VISIT THE IMPRISONED,

VISIT THE SICK,

AND BURY THE DEAD.

MAT 25:34-40, CCC 2447

CCC 2447, JN 8:7, JN 20:24-29, MAT 21:12-13

BEAR WRONGS PATIENTLY,

DO YOU LOVE ME?

FORGIVE OFFENSES WILLINGLY,

ST. VERONICA, PRAY FOR US!

COMFORT THE SORROWFUL,

AND PRAY FOR THE LIVING AND THE DEAD.

LAZARUS, COME OUT!

YOU SEE, IT'S OUR CHRISTIAN DUTY, AS DISCIPLES OF CHRIST, TO BE DISCIPLINED AND DO THESE WORKS.

THE
AIN
NG
AN
S.

PY
TH.
ED
LE.

NE
SH.

DISCIPLE (N.) BIBLICAL BORROWING FROM LATIN *DISCIPULUS*, MEANING PUPIL, STUDENT, FOLLOWER, SPECIFICALLY, A FOLLOWER OF CHRIST.

DISCIPLINE (N.) PUNISHMENT, INSTRUCTION, TRAINING, A FIELD OF STUDY. THE WORD DISCIPLINE COMES FROM *DISCIPULUS*, THE LATIN WORD FOR DISCIPLE.

EVEN THE VERY WORD "DISCIPLINE" COMES FROM THE WORD "DISCIPLE."

WE NEED A DISCIPLINED PRAYER LIFE BECAUSE PRAYING IS TALKING WITH GOD.

CCC 1816, MAT 6:5, CCC 2564-2565

IT'S SPENDING TIME WITH HIM WHOM WE LOVE AND, THEREFORE, ESSENTIAL TO OUR CHRISTIAN LIFE.

WE CAN GO TO MASS EVERY DAY, BUT MINIMALLY WE NEED TO GO TO MASS EVERY SUNDAY AND ON HOLY DAYS OF OBLIGATION.

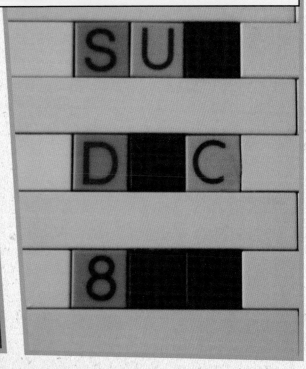

WE NEED TO UNDERSTAND THAT MASS IS NOT ABOUT BEING ENTERTAINED.

MASS IS A SACRED ENCOUNTER WITH GOD. WE ARE THERE TO WORSHIP AND PRAISE HIM, HEAR HIS WORD, AND BE UNITED WITH HIM AND RECEIVE HIS SACRAMENTAL GRACE IN HOLY COMMUNION.

LK 18:9-14, CCC 2559, MK 2:27-28, CCC 2176, CCC 1156-1158, CCC 1359-1361

THE BEST WAY TO GROW THIS RELATIONSHIP WITH GOD IS TO PARTICIPATE IN HIS SACRAMENTS. THAT WAY WE CAN BE FREED FROM SIN AND FILLED WITH HIS GRACE AND GIFTS OF THE HOLY SPIRIT!

SO WE HAVE TALKED ABOUT THE SACRAMENTS OF CHRISTIAN INITIATION: BAPTISM, CONFIRMATION, AND THE EUCHARIST, WHICH IS THE COVENANT. WE HAVE ALSO TALKED ABOUT RECONCILIATION. THAT MEANS THERE ARE THREE MORE TO GO!

THE NEXT TWO SACRAMENTS GIVE US GRACE FOR OUR STATE IN LIFE AND ARE AIMED AT SERVING OTHERS AND HELPING THEM ATTAIN SALVATION. THE FIRST ONE IS MARRIAGE.

I DIDN'T REALIZE MARRIAGE IS A SACRAMENT!

CCC 2003, CCC 2017, 1 COR 12, CCC 1212, CCC 1534, CCC 1601, EPH 5:31-32

MARRIAGE

CCC 1623, CCC 1641

IT BEGINS WITH A WEDDING (ADAM AND EVE).

JESUS' FIRST PUBLIC MIRACLE WAS AT A WEDDING (THE WEDDING FEAST AT CANA).

THE BIBLE ALSO ENDS WITH A WEDDING IN THE BOOK OF REVELATION (THE WEDDING FEAST OF THE LAMB, WHICH IS THE HOLY EUCHARIST).

ULTIMATELY, WE ARE CALLED TO AN "ETERNAL MARRIAGE." WE WILL HAVE PERFECT UNION WITH GOD FOREVER IN HEAVEN.

GEN 2:21-23, JN 2:1-8, REV 19:6-9, CCC 1027, CCC 1602, CCCC2550

IN THE BIBLE, A COMMON PLACE TO MEET YOUR SPOUSE WAS AT THE WELL.

WE ARE NO DIFFERENT. WE BECOME PART OF THE CHURCH (THE BRIDE OF CHRIST) AT THE WELL OF OUR BAPTISM.

THE BIBLE TELLS US THAT THE BRIDE AND GROOM BECOME ONE FLESH AFTER THEIR WEDDING.

AND WE BECOME ONE FLESH WITH GOD IN THE NUPTIAL UNION OF THE EUCHARIST AT OUR FIRST HOLY COMMUNION.

AFTER THE WEDDING, LIFE CONTINUES IN THIS WORLD THROUGH THE ONE-FLESH MARRIAGE UNION OF A HUSBAND AND WIFE.

GEN 24:12-14, GEN 29:1-6, EX 2:11-21, CCC 1277, MK 10:6-8, CCC 1617, CCC 1652, GEN 1:28

MARRIAGE IS A MIRROR OF THE LIFE OF THE TRINITY.

THE FATHER AND THE SON ARE ONE, AND LIFE GOES FORTH THROUGH THEIR ETERNAL LOVE, THE HOLY SPIRIT.

ST. GIANNA BERETTA MOLLA, PRAY FOR US!

IN MARRIAGE, THE HUSBAND AND WIFE ARE ONE, AND LIFE GOES FORTH THROUGH THEIR CHILDREN.

THIS IS WHY GOD COMMANDED US TO BE FRUITFUL AND MULTIPLY.

CCC 1612-1614, - CCC 1639-1640, CCC 221, CCC 1652-1654, GEN 1:28, GEN 9:7

CCC 2366-2367, CCC 2334-2335, EX 20:3, CCC 1643-1666

JP II TOTB, ECC 3:14, 1 COR 1:9, JN 15:4-5, CCC 1644, 1 SAM 2:6

IN MARRIAGE, WE ARE ASKED TO RECEIVE HIS GIFTS: CHILDREN.

SHOULD WE EVER TELL GOD "NO"?

BE IT DONE UNTO ME ACCORDING TO THY WORD.

OF COURSE NOT! SALVATION COMES THROUGH SAYING "YES."

EPH 5:25-27, CCC 1146

DID YOU KNOW THE FRONT OF THE CHURCH, THE SANCTUARY, RESEMBLES THE GROOM? CHRIST, THE GROOM, WAITS HERE FOR US TO APPROACH HIM.

AND THE PEWS, WHERE THE LAITY SIT, RESEMBLE THE BRIDE, THE CHURCH. WE PROCESS FORWARD JUST AS A BRIDE WOULD TO RECEIVE CHRIST, THE BRIDEGROOM, IN COMMUNION.

THE HIGH POINT OF THE MASS IS A WEDDING FEAST, WHERE HEAVEN CALLS US FORWARD TO RECEIVE THE BRIDEGROOM IN THE EUCHARIST.

CCC 1383, CCC 1153, CCC 777

JUST THINK ABOUT IT: WE WALK UP THE AISLE TOWARD THE ALTAR TO RECEIVE CHRIST. THE PRIEST SAYS, "BODY OF CHRIST," AND WE EACH RESPOND WITH OUR VOW, "AMEN!"

CCC 1396

THIS IS ONE REASON WHY SOME WOMEN WEAR VEILS IN CHURCH.

THEY ARE VEILED LIKE A BRIDE AT A WEDDING.

THIS POINTS TOWARD OUR UNION WITH GOD IN HEAVEN,

OUR UNION WITH GOD, WHICH BEGAN AT BAPTISM WHEN WE MET OUR SPOUSE JESUS AT THE WELL.

IF OUR VOCATION (CALLING FROM GOD) IS TO BE MARRIED, WE ONCE AGAIN PROCESS UP THE AISLE. AS BRIDE AND GROOM, WE GIVE OURSELVES TO ONE ANOTHER AT THE ALTAR OF SACRIFICE.

1 COR 11:4-10, REV 19:7-9, EZ 16:8-14, CCC 1383

For the unbelieving husband is made holy because of his wife, and the unbelieving wife is made holy because of her husband. Otherwise your children would be unclean, but as it is, they are holy.

1 Corinthians 7:14

MARRIAGE IS A SACRAMENT OF SERVICE. ITS AIM IS THE SALVATION OF OTHERS. SPOUSES ARE TO HELP EACH OTHER GET TO HEAVEN.

1 COR 7:14, CCC 1535

MARRIAGE FULLY POINTS TO ETERNITY IN HEAVEN WITH GOD WHERE WE WILL BE "ETERNALLY MARRIED TO GOD" (IN PERFECT UNION WITH GOD FOREVER).

EVEN A FUNERAL RESEMBLES MARRIAGE.

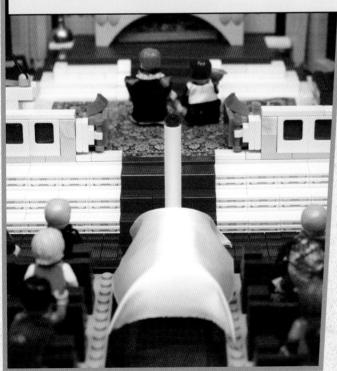

THE DECEASED PERSON IS BROUGHT UP THE AISLE ONE FINAL TIME AND VEILED BEFORE THE ALTAR OF THE LORD TO BE GIVEN IN MARRIAGE TO GOD.

MARRIAGE IS TRULY A GIFT FROM GOD THAT AIDS IN THE SALVATION OF SOULS! SPOUSES STRIVE TO HELP EACH OTHER AND THEIR CHILDREN GET TO HEAVEN.

CCC 1024, CCC 1680, CCC 1182, 1 COR 7:14

211

IN A SIMILAR WAY, PRIESTS TAKE VOWS AND ARE MARRIED TO THE CHURCH, WHICH THEY SERVE FOR THE SALVATION OF OTHERS.

AND THE CHURCH IS THE BRIDE OF CHRIST.

INRI

JUST AS EVE WAS BORN FROM THE SIDE OF ADAM, CHRIST'S BRIDE, THE CHURCH, WAS BORN FROM CHRIST'S SIDE!

BECAUSE THE PRIEST IS THE GROOM AND THE CHURCH IS THE BRIDE, HE LIVES HIS LIFE IN DEDICATION AND SUBMISSION TO HER.

212

CCC 1577, MK 3:14-19, LK 6:12-16, 1 TIM 3:1-13, 2 TIM 1:6, TIT 1:5-9, CCC 1591-1592

HOLY ORDERS

CCC 874, CCC 1536, CCC 1544

MELCHIZEDEK WAS A HIGH PRIEST IN THE OLD TESTAMENT. HE OFFERED A SACRIFICE OF BREAD AND WINE. HE WAS THE KING OF SALEM (PEACE).

CHRIST IS THE HIGH PRIEST OF HEAVEN AND EARTH WHO OFFERED HIS BODY AND BLOOD IN THE FORM OF BREAD AND WINE. HE IS THE KING OF KINGS AND THE PRINCE OF PEACE.

HEB 7:1, 1 TIM 6:15, CCC 1545

CHRIST, HOWEVER, CHOSE TO PASS HIS AUTHORITY ON TO HIS APOSTLES SO THEY COULD DISTRIBUTE HIS GRACES TO HIS PEOPLE AFTER HIS ASCENSION.

HIS GRACES ARE DISTRIBUTED THROUGH THE SACRAMENTS OF THE CHURCH BY HIS BISHOPS AND PRIESTS! CHRIST ORDAINED HIS APOSTLES TO THE HOLY PRIESTHOOD TO DISTRIBUTE HIS GRACE.

I BELIEVE ...

EVERY WEEK AT MASS, WE PROFESS THE NICENE CREED. THIS PRAYER IS A STATEMENT OF OUR FAITH.

JN 20:22-23, JN 13:1-17

Nicene Creed

I believe in one God,
the Father almighty,
maker of heaven and earth,
of all things visible and invisible.

I believe in one Lord Jesus Christ,
the Only Begotten Son of God,
born of the Father before all ages.
God from God, Light from Light,
true God from true God,
begotten, not made, consubstantial with the Father;
through him all things were made.
For us men and for our salvation
he came down from heaven,

and by the Holy Spirit was incarnate of the Virgin Mary,
and became man.

For our sake he was crucified under Pontius Pilate,
he suffered death and was buried,
and rose again on the third day
in accordance with the Scriptures.
He ascended into heaven
and is seated at the right hand of the Father.
He will come again in glory
to judge the living and the dead
and his kingdom will have no end.

I believe in the Holy Spirit, the Lord, the giver of life,
who proceeds from the Father and the Son,
who with the Father and the Son is adored and glorified,
who has spoken through the prophets.

I believe in one, holy, catholic and apostolic Church.
I confess one Baptism for the forgiveness of sins
and I look forward to the resurrection of the dead
and the life of the world to come.

Amen.

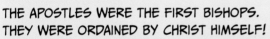

CCC 811-870, CCC 869, REV 21:14, CCC 880, MAT 16:18-19

PETER, WHO WAS ORIGINALLY NAMED SIMON, WAS AMONG THE FIRST APOSTLES CALLED BY JESUS.

SIMON PETER WAS AMONG THE FIRST CALLED BY JESUS FOR A REASON.

JESUS KNEW THAT HE WOULD FULFILL THE OLD TESTAMENT PROPHECY AND SIT IN A SEAT OF HONOR AMONG HIS PEOPLE AS THE HEAD OF HIS CHURCH, AS THE FIRST POPE.

WHAT PROPHESY FROM THE OLD TESTAMENT?

THE PROPHECY WAS FORETOLD BY THE PROPHET ISAIAH. HE DESCRIBES A KEY THAT HELD THE AUTHORITY TO RULE OVER ISRAEL, THE KINGDOM OF DAVID.

MAT 4:18-22, IS 22:23, IS 22:22

THE BIBLE TELLS US WHATEVER DOOR THIS KEY OPENS WILL REMAIN OPEN,

AND WHATEVER DOOR IT SHUTS WILL REMAIN SHUT.

THE BIBLE DESCRIBES THE AUTHORITY OF THE DAVIDIC KINGDOM AS AN IMMOVABLE PEG. IN GOD'S COVENANT WITH DAVID, HE PROMISED THAT AN ETERNAL ROYAL KINGDOM WOULD BE ESTABLISHED THROUGH HIS DESCENDANTS.

YOU SEE, FROM THE BEGINNING, GOD ALWAYS HAD A COVENANT WITH HIS PEOPLE. DO YOU REMEMBER THE OLD COVENANTS WE DISCUSSED?

YES, GOD CREATED COVENANTS WITH ADAM, NOAH, ABRAHAM, MOSES, AND DAVID.

IS 22:22-25, GEN 2:15-16, GEN 9:1-17, GEN 15:18-21, EX 19-24, 2 SAM 7:8-17

DAVID WAS BORN IN BETHLEHEM.

JESUS WAS BORN IN BETHLEHEM.

MAT 5:17, 1 SM 17:12, MAT 2:1

DAVID WAS A SHEPHERD. HE WAS ANOINTED BY THE PROPHET SAMUEL, AND THE SPIRIT OF THE LORD DESCENDED UPON HIM.

JESUS IS THE GOOD SHEPHERD. HE IS THE MESSIAH, WHICH MEANS "ANOINTED ONE." THE HOLY SPIRIT DESCENDED UPON HIM AT HIS BAPTISM IN THE JORDAN.

DAVID BECAME KING AT AGE 30.

JESUS BEGAN HIS PUBLIC MINISTRY AT AGE 30.

DAVID CAST OUT DEMONS.

JESUS CAST OUT DEMONS.

1 SAM 16:11-13, JN 10:11, JN 20:31, LK 3:22, 2 SM 5:4, JN 2:1-21, 1 SM 16:23, MAT 8:31-32

DAVID WAS BETRAYED BY HIS TRUSTED ADVISOR.

JESUS WAS BETRAYED BY HIS OWN APOSTLE, JUDAS.

DAVID WENT UP THE MOUNT OF OLIVES WEEPING.

JESUS WEPT AT THE MOUNT OF OLIVES.

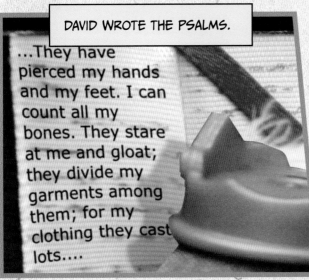

DAVID WROTE THE PSALMS.

...They have pierced my hands and my feet. I can count all my bones. They stare at me and gloat; they divide my garments among them; for my clothing they cast lots....

MY GOD, MY GOD, WHY HAVE YOU ABANDONED ME?

FROM THE CROSS, JESUS QUOTED THE PSALMS THAT SHOWED HE CAME TO FULFILL THE PROPHECIES!

PS 41:9, LK 22:1-5, 2 SM 15:30, LK 22:39-46, PS 22, MAT 27:46

DAVID WAS THE KING OF ISRAEL. HE MADE JERUSALEM THE CAPITAL CITY.

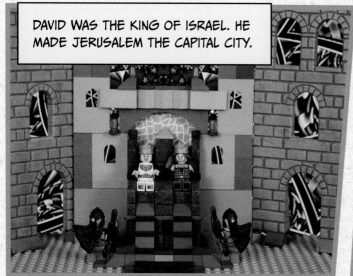

JESUS IS THE KING OF KINGS FROM THE LINE OF DAVID. HE SITS UPON THE THRONE IN THE HEAVENLY JERUSALEM.

DAVID HAD A SON, SOLOMON, WHO ALSO RULED AS KING OF JERUSALEM. SCRIPTURE CALLS HIM "A SON OF GOD," TASKED TO BUILD GOD'S TEMPLE AND RULE ON A PERPETUAL THRONE.

LIKEWISE, JESUS IS KING OF THE "HEAVENLY JERUSALEM." HE IS THE SON OF GOD AND BUILT THE TEMPLE, HIS CHURCH. THEREFORE, JESUS IS THE FULFILLMENT OF SOLOMON!

SOLOMON RODE INTO JERUSALEM ON A DONKEY.

JESUS ENTERED JERUSALEM ON A DONKEY.

2 SM 5:1-3, 1 TIM 6:16, 1 KGS 2:4, HEB 12:22, ZEC 9:9, JN 12:14-15

THE MOTHER OF SOLOMON WAS HIS QUEEN, AND HE COULD NOT REFUSE HER REQUEST.

MARY IS THE MOTHER OF JESUS AND THE QUEEN OF HEAVEN AND EARTH. JESUS DID NOT REFUSE HER REQUEST.

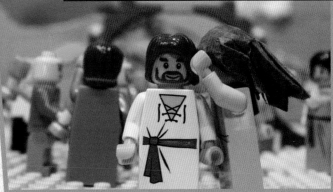

SOLOMON BUILT THE TEMPLE ON A HUGE ROCK FOUNDATION IN JERUSALEM.

JESUS CALLED SIMON "PETER," WHICH MEANS "ROCK." HE BUILT THE CATHOLIC CHURCH, THE NEW JERUSALEM, UPON THIS ROCK.

SOLOMON'S TEMPLE CONTAINED THE OLD ARK OF THE COVENANT, WHICH HELD THE TEN COMMANDMENTS (THE WORD OF GOD), THE ROD OF AARON (SYMBOLIZING THE HIGH PRIESTHOOD), AND THE MANNA (BREAD FROM HEAVEN).

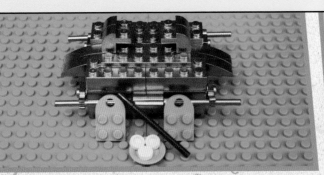

CATHOLIC CHURCHES CONTAIN TABERNACLES, WHICH HOLD THE NEW COVENANT, JESUS. HE IS THE WORD BECOME FLESH, THE HIGH PRIEST, AND THE BREAD FROM HEAVEN.

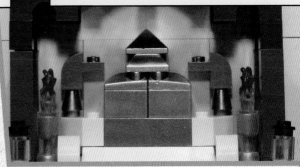

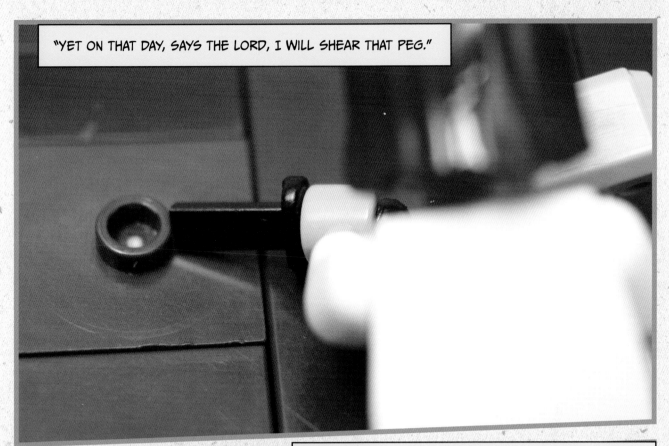

"YET ON THAT DAY, SAYS THE LORD, I WILL SHEAR THAT PEG."

SO, AS PROPHESIED, JESUS, WHO IS A DESCENDANT IN THE LINE OF DAVID, TOOK THE KEYS OF AUTHORITY OF THE DAVIDIC KINGDOM WHEN HE "SHEARED THE PEG."

ISA 22:25

THE AUTHORITY OF THE DAVIDIC KINGDOM AND THE KEYS WERE "SHEARED WITH THE PEG." CHRIST GAVE THE KEYS AND THEIR AUTHORITY TO PETER, WHO WAS PLACED IN A SEAT OF HONOR AS THE FIRST POPE OF CHRIST'S CHURCH, THE NEW JERUSALEM.

AND JUST AS AUTHORITY WAS PASSED DOWN IN THE DAVIDIC KINGDOM, PAPAL AUTHORITY HAS BEEN PASSED DOWN FROM GENERATION TO GENERATION WITHIN CHRIST'S CHURCH, WHICH WAS GIVEN THE KEYS AND BUILT ON THE ROCK JUST LIKE IN THE DAVIDIC KINGDOM.

THAT'S HOW JESUS STARTED THE CHURCH. THE FRAMEWORK FOR HIS CHURCH WAS APOSTOLIC.

WE NEED TO STAY WITHIN THAT FRAMEWORK BECAUSE...

THE BIBLE TELLS US THAT THE CHURCH IS THE PILLAR AND FOUNDATION OF TRUTH!

JESUS TOLD HIS APOSTLES, WHO WERE THE FIRST BISHOPS, THAT HE WOULD SEND THEM THE HOLY SPIRIT. THE HOLY SPIRIT WOULD LEAD THEM INTO ALL TRUTHS.

JESUS SAID, "THE FATHER HAS GIVEN ME ALL AUTHORITY IN HEAVEN AND EARTH!"

WITH THE AUTHORITY GIVEN BY THE SON, THE MISSION FROM THE FATHER, AND THE GUIDANCE OF THE HOLY SPIRIT, THE APOSTLES (BISHOPS) CONTINUED TO GROW CHRIST'S CHURCH BY ANOINTING MORE APOSTLES.

FOR EXAMPLE, AFTER JUDAS DENIED CHRIST THROUGH HIS BETRAYAL AND DEATH, PETER USED THIS AUTHORITY TO FILL THE CHAIR OF JUDAS WITH A NEW APOSTLE, MATTHIAS.

THE APOSTLES ALSO USED THIS AUTHORITY TO DRIVE OUT DEMONS IN CHRIST'S NAME.

MAT 28:18, CCC 77, ACTS 1:12-26, ACTS 16:18

SO THE APOSTLES BAPTIZED, WHICH RESTORES SANCTIFYING GRACE AND DESTROYS SIN.

THEY HEARD CONFESSIONS, WHICH RESTORES SANCTIFYING GRACE AND DESTROYS SIN.

THEY CONFIRMED, WHICH COMPLETES BAPTISM, INCREASES THE SANCTIFYING GRACE RECEIVED AT BAPTISM, AND SEALS THE SOUL WITH THE GIFTS OF THE HOLY SPIRIT.

THEY CONSECRATED THE EUCHARIST, WHICH GIVES SANCTIFYING AND ACTUAL GRACE AND DESTROYS SIN.

THEY WITNESSED MARRIAGES, WHICH GIVE SANCTIFYING AND ACTUAL GRACE.

THEY ANOINTED THE SICK, WHICH GIVES SANCTIFYING AND ACTUAL GRACE AND DESTROYS SIN.

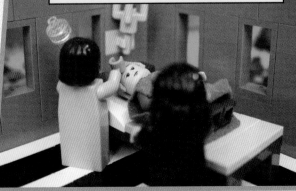

ACTS 8:36-38, ACTS 19:18, HEB 6:2, CCC 1303-1304, 1 COR 10:16, 1 COR 7:8-9, JAS 5:14

THE APOSTLES ALSO ANOINTED MORE PRIESTS TO HOLY ORDERS, WHICH GAVE THEM ACTUAL GRACE AND THE AUTHORITY TO DESTROY SIN!

THOSE PRIESTS WERE SENT ON THE SAME MISSION: TO DISTRIBUTE GRACE THROUGH CHRIST'S CHURCH AND HIS SACRAMENTS!

DID YOU KNOW THAT, AFTER JESUS ASCENDED INTO HEAVEN, A MAN NAMED SAUL WAS BRUTALLY KILLING CHRISTIANS?

ONE DAY AS SAUL WAS ON HIS WAY TO THE TOWN OF DAMASCUS, A GREAT LIGHT FROM HEAVEN SHONE UPON HIM. HE WAS SUDDENLY BLINDED AND FELL TO THE GROUND.

ST. STEPHEN, FIRST CHRISTIAN MARTYR, PRAY FOR US!

HE HEARD A VOICE SAYING, "SAUL, SAUL, WHY DO YOU PERSECUTE ME?"

THEN HE FELT SORRY FOR WHAT HE HAD DONE. SO HE CAME TO THE CHURCH.

ACTS 13:2-4, CCC 1536

242

BISHOPS (EPISCOPATE)

PRIESTS (PRESBYTERATE)

DEACONS (DIACONATE)

CCC 1554

243

CCC 1559, CCC 879

BISHOPS HAVE AUTHORITY OVER THEIR ENTIRE DIOCESE (AREA) AND ALL OF THE PRIESTS AND DEACONS IN THAT DIOCESE.

BISHOPS HAVE THE FULLNESS OF THE PRIESTHOOD,

WHICH MEANS THEY ALONE HAVE THE AUTHORITY TO OFFER ALL SEVEN OF THE SACRAMENTS ON CHRIST'S BEHALF.

ST. IGNATIUS OF ANTIOCH SAID,

WHERE THE BISHOP IS, SO TOO IS THE CATHOLIC CHURCH.

ST. IGNATIUS OF ANTIOCH, PRAY FOR US!

THIS IS BECAUSE THE CHURCH HAS THE RESPONSIBILITY TO DISTRIBUTE GOD'S GRACES THROUGH THE SACRAMENTS.

AND, ORDINARILY, IT IS A BISHOP WHO BESTOWS THE SACRAMENT OF CONFIRMATION,

ONLY BISHOPS CAN BESTOW HOLY ORDERS.

ALTHOUGH PRIESTS CAN CONFIRM WHEN SOMEONE IS IN DANGER OF DEATH OR WHEN THEY BAPTIZE OR RECEIVE AN ADULT INTO THE CHURCH.

CCC 1560, CCC 1594, CCC 1536, CCC 1536

CCC 1560-1562

CCC 1562-1568

CCC 1569-1570, CCC 1571

WE CAN ALSO SERVE THE CHURCH IN OTHER WAYS. DURING HOLY MASS, WE CAN READ THE GOSPEL, GIVE THE HOMILY, SERVE AT THE ALTAR, AND DISTRIBUTE THE HOLY EUCHARIST.

WE CAN ALSO IMPART CERTAIN BLESSINGS ON PEOPLE, EXPOSE THE BLESSED SACRAMENT FOR ADORATION, AND BLESS PEOPLE WITH THE MONSTRANCE.

THANK YOU FOR HELPING US UNDERSTAND YOUR VOCATION!

WELL, WE BETTER BE ON OUR WAY. IT'S TIME FOR ADORATION.

THANK YOU!

REMEMBER, YOU ARE NEVER TOO YOUNG TO BEGIN DISCERNING YOUR VOCATIONS! GOD BLESS YOU!

CCC 872, CCC 913, CCC 873

CCC 2560, CCC 899

BROTHERS ARE SIMILAR TO SISTERS IN THAT THEY TAKE VOWS AND LEAD LIVES OF PRAYER, SACRIFICE, AND SERVICE AMONG SOCIETY. BROTHERS ARE NOT ORDAINED WITH HOLY ORDERS.

MONKS ARE SIMILAR TO NUNS IN THAT THEY ALSO TAKE VOWS AND LEAD LIVES OF SACRIFICE, SERVICE, AND PRAYER. THEY ARE TYPICALLY CLOISTERED IN A MONASTERY AND USUALLY DON'T GO OUT INTO SOCIETY. SOME MONKS, HOWEVER, CAN ALSO BE ORDAINED WITH HOLY ORDERS AND BE A PRIEST OR DEACON.

CCC 930, CCC 920-921

CCC 935, CCC 1536

ANOINTING OF THE SICK

JN 3:16-22, CCC 1, CCC 27, CCC 1020

JN 14:1-6, CCC 1520

CCC 1514, CCC 1517

EXTREME UNCTION (ANOINTING WITH HOLY OIL),

AND VIATICUM (THE EUCHARIST).

THE OLEUM INFIRMORUM (OIL OF THE SICK) MARKS US FOR GOD AGAIN, JUST AS THE OILS USED FOR BAPTISM AND CONFIRMATION PLACED AN INDELIBLE MARK ON OUR SOUL. ALL THREE OF THESE OILS ARE BLESSED BY THE BISHOP ON HOLY THURSDAY.

CCC 1517, CCC 1524-1525, CCC 1512, CCC 1297

ST. JOSEPH WAS CHOSEN BY GOD TO CARE AND INTERCEDE FOR JESUS AND MARY,

AND AT THE END OF HIS LIFE, HE DIED IN THE ARMS OF JESUS AND MARY.

IF WE HAVE A DEVOTION TO HIM, HE CAN ADVOCATE FOR US, AS WELL.

HE IS KNOWN AS THE TERROR OF DEMONS!

ST. JOSEPH, PRAY FOR US!

CCC 1523

CCC 1523, CCC 1520

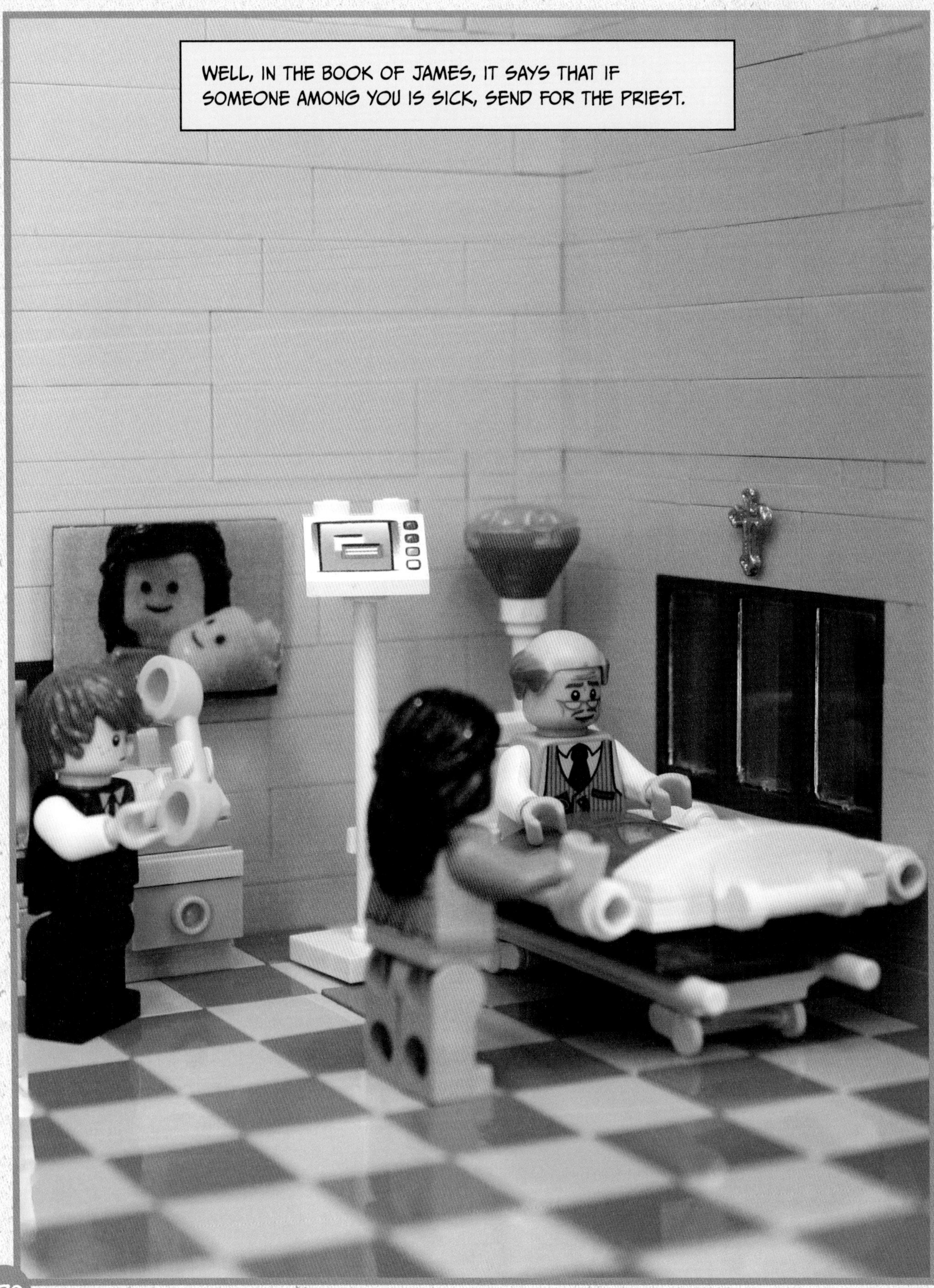
WELL, IN THE BOOK OF JAMES, IT SAYS THAT IF SOMEONE AMONG YOU IS SICK, SEND FOR THE PRIEST.

JAMES 5:14-15

REMEMBER, ANOINTING OF THE SICK HAS THREE PARTS: PENANCE, EXTREME UNCTION, AND VIATICUM.

FIRST, THE PRIEST OFFERS **PENANCE** (RECONCILIATION), WHICH IS WHEN THE PRIEST HEARS CONFESSION AND GIVES ABSOLUTION.

NEXT, THE PRIEST ADMINISTERS **EXTREME UNCTION**, WHICH IS WHEN HE PRAYS OVER THE SICK PERSON AND ANOINTS HIM OR HER WITH OLEUM INFIRMORUM (OIL OF THE SICK).

FINALLY, THE PRIEST ADMINISTERS **VIATICUM** (THE EUCHARIST), WHICH IS BREAD FOR THE JOURNEY.

IT'S CERTAINLY POSSIBLE THAT THIS SACRAMENT CAN BRING PHYSICAL HEALING. BUT LIKE ALL OF THE SACRAMENTS, THE MOST IMPORTANT HEALING IS SPIRITUAL.

DOES THAT HEAL THE PERSON'S SICKNESS?

JESUS DEMONSTRATES THIS IN THE NEW TESTAMENT. LEPERS SUFFERED FROM A DESTRUCTIVE DISEASE.

IN FACT, IT WAS SO DANGEROUS, THEY HAD TO BE REMOVED FROM THE COMMUNITY.

REMEMBER, THAT'S EXACTLY WHAT SIN DOES TO US: IT REMOVES US FROM GOD'S COMMUNITY.

WHEN JESUS HEALED THE LEPERS, HE SHOWED US A PHYSICAL TRUTH AND AN EVEN GREATER SPIRITUAL TRUTH!

CCC 1503, MAT 8:1-4, NUM 5:2, GEN 3:23, LK 17:11-19

LK 17:11-19, LK 5:23, CCC 1524-1525

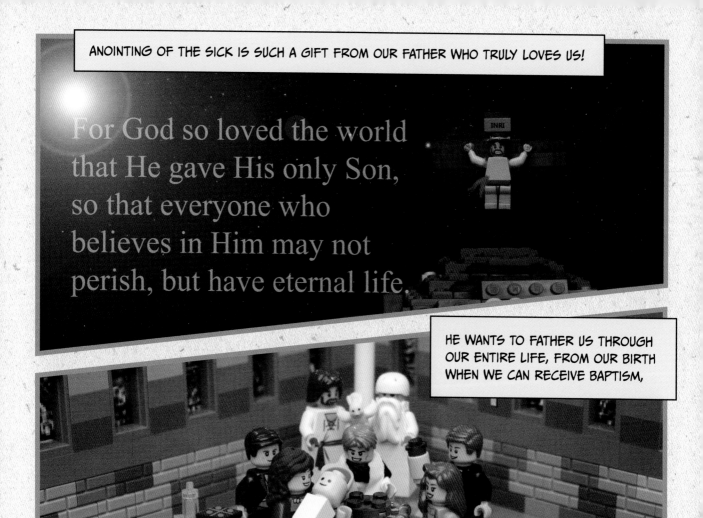

ANOINTING OF THE SICK IS SUCH A GIFT FROM OUR FATHER WHO TRULY LOVES US!

For God so loved the world that He gave His only Son, so that everyone who believes in Him may not perish, but have eternal life.

HE WANTS TO FATHER US THROUGH OUR ENTIRE LIFE, FROM OUR BIRTH WHEN WE CAN RECEIVE BAPTISM,

ALL THE WAY THROUGH TO OUR DEATH WHEN WE CAN RECEIVE ANOINTING OF THE SICK. HE GAVE US THE SACRAMENTS SO WE CAN DRAW NEAR TO HIM AND ULTIMATELY BE ETERNALLY UNITED WITH HIM!

JN 3:16, CCC 1525

ANOINTING OF THE SICK OFFERS REMISSION OF THE ETERNAL PUNISHMENT (HELL) INCURRED BY MORTAL SIN.

IT CAN ALSO REMOVE TEMPORAL PUNISHMENT (PURGATORY) FOR SIN AND GIVE US STRENGTH TO ENDURE THE FINAL BATTLE FOR OUR ETERNAL SOUL.

OR, IF IT'S GOD'S WILL, IT CAN RESTORE THE BODY TO HEALTH!

CCC 1510, CCC 1523, CCC 1532, CCC 1506

BISHOP FULTON SHEEN TELLS US,

SIN ENTERS THE BODY THROUGH OUR SENSES (EYES, EARS, NOSE, MOUTH, HANDS, AND FEET) ...

VEN. ARCHBISHOP FULTON J. SHEEN, PRAY FOR US!

"... THAT IS WHY THE HEAD AND HANDS ARE ANOINTED AND OTHER PARTS OF THE BODY MAY BE ANOINTED DURING EXTREME UNCTION."

1 COR 11:29-31, CCC 1513

"JUST AS A CHIMNEY GETS DIRTY FROM THE SOOT LEFT BEHIND,"

"OUR BODY CAN MANIFEST SIN IN THE FORM OF AILMENTS AND DISEASE."

"AND THE ANOINTING OF THE SICK CAN REMOVE SIN AND CLEANSE OUR BODY TO RESTORE HEALTH. BUT MOST IMPORTANTLY,"

"THIS SACRAMENT RESTORES OUR **SPIRITUAL HEALTH** AND OUR RELATIONSHIP WITH GOD!"

OUR SALVATION WAS PURCHASED BY CHRIST'S SUFFERING AND DEATH ON THE CROSS.

INRI

1 COR 11:29-31, CCC 1502, CCC 1526, 1 COR 6:20

TO RECEIVE SALVATION, WE HAVE TO CONFORM OUR LIFE AND OUR WILL TO GOD'S PERFECT WILL AND TRUST IN HIS DIVINE MERCY! THERE IS NO BETTER WAY TO ACCOMPLISH THIS THAN TO LIVE A SACRAMENTAL RELATIONSHIP WITH JESUS CHRIST, JUST AS HE INSTRUCTED! ONCE WE RECEIVE THE SACRAMENTS OF INITIATION—**BAPTISM, CONFIRMATION,** AND THE **HOLY EUCHARIST**—WE CONTINUE TO GROW IN GRACE FOR OUR STATE IN LIFE THROUGH THE SACRAMENTS OF SERVICE: **MARRIAGE** AND **HOLY ORDERS.** AND WE CAN RECEIVE CONTINUOUS HEALING AND GRACE THROUGH THE SACRAMENTS OF HEALING: **RECONCILIATION** AND **ANOINTING OF THE SICK.**

ST. FAUSTINA KOWALSKA, PRAY FOR US!

CCC 1113, CCC 1134

CCC 402, CCC 1392-1393

280

REV 21:27, CCC 830

ABRAM/ABRAHAM—Born in the twentieth or nineteenth century B.C., in Ur of the Chaldeans on the Euphrates River. His father, Terah, named him Abram. The family migrated to Haran, where Terah died (Genesis 11:26-31). At God's behest, Abram, his wife, Sarah, his nephew, Lot, and all their followers moved on to Canaan (Genesis 12:4). When Abram was ninety-nine years old, God made a covenant with him, changing his name to Abraham and promising to make him the "father of a multitude of nations ... [Genesis 17:1-5] I will make you into nations and your issue shall be kings ... I will give to you and your descendants the land you are living in, the whole land of Canaan, to own in perpetuity, and I will be your God" (Genesis 17:5-8). Hence he has been called the founder of the Hebrew people. Abraham's dedication to the will of God was tested when he was told to take his son, Isaac, to the land of Moriah (which later became the site of the Jerusalem temple) and sacrifice his son as a burnt offering. He obeyed without hesitation, but Isaac was spared at the last moment (Genesis 22). In his final days Abraham arranged to have his son marry Rebekah, one of his kinfolk (Genesis 24), and left Isaac all his possessions before he died at the age of one hundred seventy-five (Genesis 25).

ABSOLUTION—In the sacrament of penance, the act by which a qualified priest, having the necessary jurisdiction, remits the guilt and penalty due to sin. The new formula of absolution, since the Second Vatican Council, is: "God, the Father of mercies, through the death and resurrection of His Son, has reconciled the world to Himself and sent the Holy Spirit among us for the forgiveness of sins; through the ministry of the Church may God give you pardon and peace, and I absolve you from your sins in the name of the Father, and of the Son, and of the Holy Spirit." To which the penitent answers, "Amen." In this formula essential words are: "I absolve you." For centuries, the Church used the deprecatory form of absolution, e.g., "May God absolve you from your sins." This was really declarative in meaning, as is clear from the fact that in the whole of tradition the priest who absolved was looked upon as a judge who actually absolved, even though he used the subjunctive mood to express his affirmative judgment. (Etym. Latin *absolvere*, to free from; to absolve, acquit.)

ACTUAL SIN—Any thought, word, deed, or omission contrary to God's eternal law. All actual sins are classified on the basis of this division, where sinful thoughts are essentially desires, the words may either be spoken or otherwise articulated, the deeds involve some external manifestation, and omissions are failures to do what should have been done by a person in a given set of circumstances.

Sin is a human act that presumes three elements: objective malice in the action performed, or at least the person considers it wrong; actual advertence of mind by which the sinner is at least confusedly aware of the malice of his conduct; and consent of the will, which formally constitutes actual sin and without which the sin is said to be only material.

Every sin is a genuine offense against God. There is consequently no such thing as merely philosophical sin, which offends against right reason but is not at the same time a deliberate transgression of the divine law. Sin is theological by its very nature.

ADORATION—Acknowledgement that, because the whole Christ is really present in the Blessed Sacrament, he is to be adored in the Eucharist as the incarnate God. The manner of showing this homage differs among countries and has varied through the ages. The postcouncilliar legislation for the Latin Rite requires that the Blessed Sacrament, whether in the tabernacle or exposed on the altar, is to be venerated by genuflecting on one knee.

ANOINTING OF THE SICK—Sacrament of the New Law, instituted by Christ to give the sick spiritual aid and strength and to perfect spiritual health, including, if need be, the remission of sins. Conditionally it also restores bodily health to Christians who are seriously ill. It consists essentially in the anointing by a priest of the forehead and the hands, while pronouncing the words "Through this holy anointing and His most loving mercy, may the Lord assist you by the grace of the Holy Spirit, so that, freed from your sins, He may save you and in His goodness raise you up." In case of necessity, a single anointing of the forehead or of another suitable part of the body suffices. Olive oil, blessed by a bishop, is normally used for the anointing, but any vegetable oil may be substituted in case of emergency.

The institution of anointing by Christ is an article of the Catholic faith, defined by the Council of Trent (Denzinger 1716). The Church further teaches that this sacrament is implied in Gospel reference to Christ sending out the disciples, who "anointed many sick people with oil and cured them" (Mark 6:13); moreover that the sacrament was promulgated by the Apostle James when he wrote, "Is anyone among you sick? Let him bring in the presbyters of the Church and let them pray over him, anointing him with oil in the name of the Lord. And the prayer of faith will save the sick man and the Lord will raise him up and if he be in sins, they shall be forgiven him" (James 5:14-15).

ASCENSION—Christ's going up to heaven forty days after his resurrection from the dead. All the creeds affirm the fact, and the Church teaches that he ascended into heaven in body and soul (Denzinger 801). He ascended into heaven by his own power, as God in divine power and as man in the power of his transfigured soul, which moves his transfigured body, as it will. In regard to the human nature of Christ, one can also say, with the Scriptures, that it was taken up or elevated into heaven by God (Mark 16:19; Luke 24:51; Acts 1:9, 11).

Rationalism has denied the doctrine since the earliest times, e.g., Celsus in the second century. It tries to explain the Ascension as a borrowing from the Old Testament or from pagan mythology, but in doing so omits the basic differences.

Doctrinally the Ascension means the final elevation of Christ's human nature into the condition of divine glory. It is the concluding work of redemption. According to the Church's common teaching, the souls of the just from the pre-Christian era went with the Savior into the glory of heaven. Christ's Ascension is the archetype and pledge of our own ascension into heaven. (Etym. Latin *ascensio*, an ascending, ascent.)

ASSUMPTION—The doctrine of Mary's entrance into heaven, body and soul. As defined by Pope Pius XII in 1950, the dogma declares that "Mary, the immaculate perpetually Virgin Mother of God, after the completion of her earthly life, was assumed body and soul into the glory of heaven."

While there is no direct evidence of the Assumption in the Bible, implicitly the Church argues from Mary's fullness of grace (Luke 1:28). Since she was full of grace, she remained preserved from the consequence of sin, namely corruption of the body after death and postponement of bodily happiness in heaven until the last day.

The Church does not rely on the Scriptures for belief in Mary's Assumption. The doctrine is rather part of the oral tradition, handed down over the centuries. It was therefore certainly revealed because, in reply to the questions, the Catholic bishops of the world all but unanimously expressed the belief that this was part of the divine revelations. In explaining the grounds for the Church's belief, Pius XII singled out the fact that Mary was the Mother of God; as the body of Christ originated from the body of Mary (*caro Jesu est caro Mariae*); that her body was preserved unimpaired in virginal integrity, and therefore it was fitting that it should not be subject to destruction after death; and that since Mary so closely shared in Christ's redemptive mission on earth, she deserved to join him also in bodily glorification.

BAPTISM—The sacrament in which, by water and the word of God, a person is cleansed of all sin and reborn and sanctified in Christ to everlasting life. (Etym. Latin *baptisma*; from Greek *baptisma*, a dipping.)

BRIDE OF CHRIST—See SPOUSE OF CHRIST

CHRISM—A consecrated mixture of olive oil and balsam. Blessed by a bishop, it is used in the public administration of baptism, confirmation, and holy orders; in the blessing of tower bells, baptismal water, and in the consecration of churches, altars, chalices, and patens. (Etym. Middle English *chrisom*, short for chrism cloth.)

CLOISTER—A covered walk enclosing a quadrangle around which monasteries are built. Also an enclosure for religious retirement. In canon law, restrictions to the free entry of outsiders within the limits of certain areas of the residences of men or women religious. (Etym. Latin *claustrum*, enclosure.)

COMMUNION OF SAINTS—The unity and cooperation of the members of the Church on earth with those in heaven and in purgatory. They are united as being one Mystical Body of Christ. The faithful on earth are in communion with each other by professing the same faith, obeying the same authority, and assisting each other with their prayers and good works. They are in communion with the saints in heaven by honoring them as glorified members of the Church, invoking their prayers and aid, and striving to imitate their virtues. They are in communion with the souls in purgatory by helping them with their prayers and good works.

CONFESSION, SACRAMENT OF—See PENANCE

CONFIRMATION—The sacrament in which, through the laying on of hands, anointing with chrism, and prayer, those already baptized are strengthened by the Holy Spirit in order that they may steadfastly profess the faith and faithfully live up to their profession. Confirmation is not strictly necessary for salvation, but it is eminently important in contributing to Christian perfection and there is a grave obligation to receive it in due time. (Etym. Latin con-, thoroughly + firmare, to make firm: confirmatio, fortification, strengthening.)

CORPORAL WORKS OF MERCY—The seven practices of charity, based on Christ's prediction of the Last Judgment (Matthew 5:3-10) that will determine each person's final destiny. They are: 1. to feed the hungry; 2. to give drink to the thirsty; 3. to clothe the naked; 4. to shelter the homeless; 5. to visit the sick; 6. to visit those in prison; and 7. to bury the dead.

COVENANT—In the Old Testament an agreement between God and Israel in which God promised protection to the Chosen People in return for exclusive loyalty. "If you obey my voice and hold fast to my covenant, you of all nations will be my very own" (Exodus 19:5). Moses presented Yahweh's offer to his people, who promptly "answered as one, 'All that Yahweh has said we will do.'" The compact was sealed (Exodus 19:8). Many years later Jeremiah prophesied that a new covenant would be offered. "Deep within them," Yahweh promised, "I will plant my law, writing it on their hearts" (Jeremiah 31:31-34). Ezekiel foresaw that God would "make a covenant of peace with them, an eternal covenant" (Ezekiel 37:26). Its universal character was foreshadowed by Isaiah, to whom it was revealed by Yahweh, "so that my salvation may reach to the ends of the earth" (Isaiah 49:6). In the New Testament, when Paul was explaining to the Corinthians the institution of the Eucharist at the Last Supper, he repeated Christ's words: "This cup is the new covenant in my blood, Whenever you drink it, do this as a memorial of me" (I Corinthians 11:25). This master idea of the New Testament is reinforced in the Letter to the Hebrews: "It follows that it is a greater covenant for which Jesus has become our guarantee" (Hebrews 7:22). Christ himself is the new covenant between God and his people. (Etym. Latin convenire, to agree, to come together.)

DISCIPLES—One who is learning or has learned. In the New Testament the word describes any follower of Jesus' teaching (Matthew 10:1). During his public ministry it referred as well to his twelve chosen aides, but in the Acts of the Apostles they are always referred to as Apostles (Acts 1:26). (Etym. Latin discipulus, pupil, follower.)

EASTER—The day commemorating Christ's Resurrection from the dead. It is the greatest of all Christian festivals, having the central place in the liturgical year. It is the Christian feast linked with the Jewish Pasch. The exultant Alleluia is constantly repeated in the Mass and Divine Office, the Vidi Aquam replaces the Asperges, and the Regina Coeli the Angelus. The Easter season continues from Easter Sunday to Trinity Sunday inclusive. (Etym. Anglo-Saxon Eastre, Teutonic goddess of dawn and spring.)

EDEN—The beautiful garden in which God put Adam and Eve. After they disobeyed him, they were expelled (Genesis 2, 3). It is a word used in Scripture to suggest an ideal place to live (Isaiah 51:3; Ezekiel 31:9).

EMMAUS—A village about seven miles from Jerusalem. It was on the road to Emmaus that two disciples met the risen Jesus and accompanied him to the village (Luke 24:13-35). Not until he broke bread at supper did they recognize him. Then he disappeared and they hastened back to Jerusalem to tell the Apostles of the encounter.

EUCHARIST—The true Body and Blood of Jesus Christ, who is really and substantially present under the appearances of bread and wine, in order to offer himself in the sacrifice of the Mass and to be received as spiritual food in Holy Communion. It is called Eucharist, or "thanksgiving," because at its institution at the Last Supper Christ "gave thanks," and by this fact it is the supreme object and act of Christian gratitude to God.

Although the same name is used, the Eucharist is any one or all three aspects of one mystery, namely the Real Presence, the Sacrifice, and Communion. As Real Presence, the Eucharist is Christ in his abiding existence on earth today; as Sacrifice, it is Christ in his abiding action of High Priest, continuing now to communicate the graces he merited on Calvary; and as Communion, it is Christ coming to enlighten and strengthen the believer by nourishing his soul for eternal life. (Etym. Latin eucharistia, the virtue of thanksgiving or thankfulness; from Greek eucharistia, gratitude; from eu-, good + charizesthai, to show favor.)

EXAMINATION OF CONSCIENCE — Reflection in God's presence on one's state of soul, e.g., in preparation for the sacrament of penance.

EXTREME UNCTION—See ANOINTING OF THE SICK

FRUITS OF THE HOLY SPIRIT—Supernatural works that, according to St. Paul, manifest the presence of the Holy Spirit. The one who performs them recognizes God's presence by the happiness he experiences, and others the divine presence by witnessing these good works (Galatians 5:22-23). They are, in other words, identifiable effects of the Holy Spirit. In the Vulgate text they are: charity, joy, peace, patience, benignity, goodness, longanimity, mildness, faith, modesty, continency, and chastity.

GENUFLECT—Bending of the knee as an act of reverence. Customary when passing before the Blessed Sacrament in the tabernacle, entering the pew for divine worship, and during certain ceremonies to the Cross. A double genuflection of both knees simultaneously was commonly made before the Blessed Sacrament exposed in a monstrance. The new directive since the Second Vatican Council specifies: "One knee is bent before the Blessed Sacrament, whether reserved in the tabernacle or exposed for public adoration" (*Eucharistiae Sacramentum*, 1973, number 84). Genuflections are also made to the Pope, to a cardinal, and to a bishop in his own diocese.

GETHSEMANE—The garden lying outside Jerusalem on the Mount of Olives where Jesus spent the agonizing hours praying prior to his arrest (Mark 14:32-52, John 18:1-12). (Etym. Aramaic *gat semane*, oil press; Greek *gethsēmanei*.)

GIFTS OF THE HOLY SPIRIT—The seven forms of supernatural initiative conferred with the reception of sanctifying grace. They are in the nature of supernatural reflexes, or reactive instincts, that spontaneously answer to the divine impulses of grace almost without reflection but always with full consent. The gifts are wisdom (*sapientia*), understanding (*intellectus*), knowledge (*scientia*), fortitude or courage (*fortitudo*), counsel (*consilium*), piety or love (*pietas*), and fear of the Lord (*timor Domini*).

GODPARENT—Sponsors who make profession of faith for the person being baptized. Solemn baptism requires godparents. The godparent assumes an obligation to instruct the child in the event of the death or neglect of the parents, in order to fulfill the baptismal promises. Being a godparent creates a spiritual relationship that is recognized in ecclesiastical law.

GRAVE SIN—The transgression of a divine law in a grievous matter with full knowledge and consent.

The matter may be serious either in itself (as blasphemy) or because of the circumstances (as striking one's father or mother) or on account of its purpose (as telling a lie in order to destroy a person's character). Sufficient knowledge of the serious nature of a sinful action is present if one is clearly conscious that the act is mortally sinful, say because the Scriptures or the Church identify certain acts as seriously offensive to God. It is enough that one knows that what one intends to do may be a mortal sin, but does it anyhow. Indifference to the laws of God is equivalent to disobeying them.

Full consent is present when one freely wills to commit an action although one clearly knows it is gravely sinful. No sin is committed if one does not will the deed, no matter how clear one's knowledge may be. After all, the essence of sin is in the free will. Thus, too, a person does not sin who, with the best of will, cannot dispel obscene or blasphemous thoughts and desires, even though he or she well knows they are gravely sinful. The resolution to perform an action is not the same as the pleasure or satisfaction experienced in the emotions, nor the same as a compulsive idea, "I like the sin." One sign of partial knowledge or not full consent would be the fact that a person does not complete an action when this can easily be done, or is so minded that the person would rather die than commit a grave sin.

HELL—The place and state of eternal punishment for the fallen angels and human beings who die deliberately estranged from the love of God. There is a twofold punishment in hell: the pain of loss, which consists in the deprivation of the vision of God, and the pain of sense, which consists in the suffering caused by outside material things. The punishment of hell is eternal, as declared by Christ in his prediction of the last day (Matthew 25:46), and as defined by the Fourth Lateran Council, stating that the wicked will "receive a perpetual punishment with the devil" (Denzinger 801). The existence of hell is consistent with divine justice, since God respects human freedom and those who are lost actually condemn themselves by their resistance to the grace of God.

HOLY DAYS OF OBLIGATION—Feast days to be observed by attendance at Mass and rest, as far as possible, from unnecessary servile work. The number and dates of these vary among countries. In the United States there are six holy days: Solemnity of Mary on January 1; Ascension of Our Lord, forty days after Easter; Assumption of the Blessed Virgin, August 15; All Saints' Day, November 1; Mary's Immaculate Conception, December 8; and Christmas, or the birth of Christ, December 25. On holy days the pastor of every parish is required to offer or have offered a special Mass for his parishioners.

HOLY ORDERS—See ORDERS, SACRAMENT OF

HYSSOP—A plant of unknown identity, mentioned in the Scriptures. Found in Egypt, Sinai, and Canaan, it was used to sprinkle the blood of the paschal lamb or victims of sacrifice. It is referred to in the Psalm Miserere and in the Church's prayers.

JERUSALEM—Ancient city in Palestine, the religious and political center of the Jewish people, situated on the crest of a chain of mountains that cross Palestine from north to south. Originally called Salem, it was the capital of King Melchizedek about 2100 B.C. (Genesis 14). First mentioned in the Book of Joshua (10, 15), the inhabitants were known as Jebusites. When the Promised Land was parceled out, Jerusalem was assigned to the tribe of Benjamin. Its most famous rulers were King David, who brought the Ark of the Covenant into the city, and his son Solomon, who built the first Temple. A second Temple was built in the sixth century B.C., and the third (and last) was the work of Herod the Great, who ruled as a vassal of Rome from 37 to 4 B.C. The Christian history of Jerusalem begins with the short ministry of the Savior, culminating in his death, resurrection, and ascension. The Apostles lived and taught there for some time after Pentecost, and met in Jerusalem for their first council about A.D. 49. The Apostle St. James the Less was the first Bishop of Jerusalem, where he was condemned by the Sanhedrin and martyred in A.D. 62.

JEWS—Those who adhere to Judaism both as a religion and a people. Originally the name was restricted to the subjects of the kingdom of Judah. But after the Babylonian exile it became the common name for the race descended from Jacob and for the followers of the Mosaic religion.

LAST RITES—See **ANOINTING OF THE SICK**

LAST SUPPER—The last meal taken by Christ with his apostles, the night before his Passion. On this occasion he instituted the Holy Eucharist and the priesthood, and gave the apostles the long discourse on the Trinity and Christian charity, as recorded by St. John. He then proceeded to Gethsemane and the Agony in the Garden.

MANNA—The name given in Scripture for the miraculous food sent to the Israelites in the desert (Exodus 16:4-36). There are natural exudates from trees and shrubs in Arabia that yield, during two months in the fall, a minute quantity of edible substance. But their limited supply, with characteristic taste, makes them totally unlike what the Bible describes as the manna of the Exodus.

MARRIAGE—See MATRIMONY

MATRIMONY—Marriage, but a more appropriate term for legal and religious use. It is the proper term for the sacrament of marriage, and refers more to the relationship between husband and wife than to the ceremony or the state of marriage.

MELCHIZEDEK—A king of Salem and a priest. When Abraham returned from battle after rescuing Lot, Melchizedek greeted him and gave him a blessing in honor of his victory (Genesis 14:18-20). In return Abraham offered him tithes because of his priesthood. In a Psalm devoted to the dual role of priest and king, David exclaimed, "Yahweh has sworn an oath which he never will retract, You are a priest of the order of Melchizedek and forever" (Psalm 110:4). There are only two references to this priest-king in the Old Testament. In the New Testament the Epistle to the Hebrews associates Christ's priesthood with Melchizedek's by quoting in three successive chapters the invocation from Psalm 110: "You are a priest of the order of Melchizedek and forever." This is also the biblical basis for the Catholic doctrine that, once a man is ordained a priest, his priesthood, like Christ's "in the line of Melchizedek," is forever (Hebrews 5, 6, 7).

MERCY—The disposition to be kind and forgiving. Founded on compassion, mercy differs from compassion or the feeling of sympathy in putting this feeling into practice with a readiness to assist. It is therefore the ready willingness to help anyone in need, especially in need of pardon or reconciliation.

MESSIAH—The Hebrew word for "Anointed One." The equivalent word in Greek is Christos. In the Old Testament it was sometimes applied in a general sense to prophets or priests (Exodus 30:30), but more specifically it referred to the coming of one who would usher in a period of righteousness and conquer sin and evil (Daniel 9:26). In the New Testament the Evangelists made it clear that they knew Jesus was the long-anticipated Messiah (Acts 2:36; Matthew 16:17; Galatians 3:24-29). Those who refused to accept Jesus interpreted the promised kingdom to be a worldly domain and looked forward to a messiah who would be a military leader to help Israel triumph over her enemies.

MONSTRANCE—A symbol of the Blessed Sacrament since the monstrance is the sacred vessel which contains the consecrated Host when exposed or carried in procession. It is a well-known emblem of St. Clare, who is reported to have repulsed unbelievers who assaulted her convent of nuns by presenting to their gaze Christ in the monstrance. St. Peter Julian Eymard, founder of the Blessed Sacrament Fathers, is symbolized carrying the monstrance and blessing the people with it. St. Thomas Aquinas has the monstrance among his many emblems as the author of the famous hymns "Lauda Sion and Pange Lingua," written to honor the Eucharistic Lord. St. John Neumann, who first established the forty hours' devotion in America, and St. Paschal Baylon, patron of Eucharistic Congresses, are both represented in art with the monstrance. (Etym. Latin monstrans, from monstrare, to show, point out, indicate.)

MORTAL SIN—An actual sin that destroys sanctifying grace and causes the supernatural death of the soul. Mortal sin is a turning away from God because of seriously inordinate adherence to creatures that causes grave injury to a person's rational nature and to the social order, and deprives the sinner of a right to heaven.

The terms mortal, deadly, grave, and serious applied to sin are synonyms, each with a slightly different implication. Mortal and deadly focus on the effects in the sinner, namely deprivation of the state of friendship with God; grave and serious refer to the importance of the matter in which a person offends God. But the Church never distinguishes among these terms as though they represented different kinds of sins. There is only one recognized correlative to mortal sin, and that is venial sin, which offends against God but does not cause the loss of one's state of grace. (Etym. Latin *mors*, death.)

MOSES—The greatest figure in the Old Testament, the founder of Israel, lawgiver, leader, and proponent of monotheism. Of the tribe of Levi, he was born in Egypt during a persecution when all the Hebrew male children were to be killed. Exposed on the Nile, he was rescued by Pharaoh's daughter and educated at court. God appeared to him in a burning bush and told him to deliver his people with the help of Aaron. The plagues did not make Pharaoh relent, until the death of every firstborn forced him to yield. Moses then led the Israelites through the years' long exodus, but he is excluded from the Promised Land because of his lack of confidence at the "Waters of Contradiction." The prophet died on Mount Nebo after pronouncing the three memorable discourses preserved in Deuteronomy. He was buried in the valley of Moab, but no one knows where.

NEW JERUSALEM—In biblical language the Heavenly City of the angels and saints after the Last Day. As described by St. John in the prophetic vision: "I saw the holy city, and the New Jerusalem coming down from God out of heaven, as beautiful as a bride all dressed for her husband" (Apocalypse 21:2).

NICENE CREED—There are two creeds that have the same name. The original Nicene Creed was issued in A.D. 325 by the Council of Nicaea. It was composed by the Fathers of the Council in their conflict with Arianism and contains the term *homoousios* (consubstantial). It is comparatively short, ends with the phrase, "and in the Holy Spirit," and has attached to it four anathemas against Arianism. The more common Nicene Creed is more accurately the Nicene-Constantinople Creed. It came after the first ecumenical Council of Constantinople (381), is the creed now used in the liturgy, including the added phrases "and the Son," and "died," and differs from the preceding in that it: 1. has more about the person of Christ; 2. omits the phrase "from the substance of the Father" after homoousios; 3. says more about the Holy Spirit; 4. adds the articles on the Church, baptism, the resurrection, and eternal life; and 5. contains no anathemas. The full text reads: "I believe in one God, the Father almighty, maker of heaven and earth, of all things visible and invisible. I believe in one Lord, Jesus Christ, the Only-Begotten Son of God, born of the Father before all ages. God from God, Light from Light, true God from true God, begotten, not made, consubstantial with the Father; through him all things were made. For us men and for our salvation he came down from heaven, and by the Holy Spirit was incarnate of the Virgin Mary, and became man. For our sake he was crucified under Pontius Pilate, he suffered death and was buried, and rose again on the third day in accordance with the Scriptures. He ascended into heaven and is seated at the right hand of the Father. He will come again in glory to judge the living and the dead and his kingdom will have no end. I believe in the Holy Spirit, the Lord, the giver of life, who proceeds from the Father and the Son, who with the Father and the Son is adored and glorified, who has spoken through the prophets. I believe in one, holy, catholic and apostolic Church. I confess one Baptism for the forgiveness of sins and I look forward to the resurrection of the dead and the life of the world to come. Amen."

NOAH—Son of Lamech and father of Shem, Ham, and Japheth. Yahweh was so embittered by the corruption and faithlessness of the world that he decided he would wipe out the human race in a flood. The one exception he made was Noah and his family. He gave Noah detailed instructions about the construction of an ark strong enough to remain intact (Genesis 6). Then he instructed him to take aboard his family and two specimens of every kind of animal and bird, male and female, so that after the flood the world could be repopulated. Noah obeyed Yahweh. Every living being outside the ark was destroyed when the flood submerged the earth (Genesis 7). After several months Noah had proof that the waters receded enough for all to leave the ark, which was now resting on Mount Ararat (Genesis 8). God promised, "Never again will I strike down every living being . . ." (Genesis 8:21). "There shall be no flood to destroy the earth again" (Genesis 9:11). Noah's sons became the eponymous ancestors of the great races in the repopulation of the world.

OIL OF THE SICK—The olive oil blessed by the bishop of a diocese for use in the sacrament of anointing of the sick. Commonly abbreviated O.I. (*oleum infirmorum*, oil of the sick) on oil stocks used by priests. Until 1874, when

Pope Paul VI published the new Order of Anointing the Sick, olive oil was prescribed for the valid administration of the sacrament. This is no longer necessary. Any oil from plants is permissible in case of necessity; and the blessing by a bishop, though ordinarily required, may now be supplied by a duly authorized priest and, in emergency, by any priest.

OLD TESTAMENT—A term denoting the time from the origin of the human race to Christ; also the primitive, patriarchal, and prophetic revelation; and the Old Covenant of Yahweh with the Israelites. But most commonly, the Old Testament means the collection of books that the Catholic Church believes are divinely inspired, and that are not the New Testament. In biblical order they are: Genesis, Exodus, Leviticus, Numbers, Deuteronomy, Joshua, Judges, Ruth, I and II Samuel, I and II Kings, I and II Chronicles, Ezra, Nehemiah, Tobit, Judith, Esther, I and II Maccabees, Job, Psalms, Proverbs, Ecclesiastes, Isaiah, Jeremiah, Lamentations, Baruch, Ezekiel, Daniel, Hosea, Joel, Amos, Obadiah, Jonah, Micah, Nahum, Habakkuk, Zephaniah, Haggai, Zechariah, and Malachi.

ORDERS, SACRAMENT OF — The sacrament that, by the imposition of a bishop's hands, confers on a man the grace and spiritual power to sanctify others. There are three forms of this sacrament, also called sacramental orders, namely diaconate, priesthood and episcopate. They are not, however, three sacraments, but only one sacrament that is separately administered with three successively higher sacramental effects. It is certain that every baptized male can be validly ordained, although it would be highly illicit to ordain him before the age of reason. It is likewise certain that every baptized male can be validly ordained a priest without previously being ordained a deacon. However, the more probable teaching is that a baptized male cannot be validly consecrated a bishop unless he has previously been ordained a priest.

ORIGINAL SIN—Either the sin committed by Adam as the head of the human race, or the sin he passed onto his posterity with which every human being, with the certain exception of Christ and his Mother, is conceived and born. The sin of Adam is called originating original sin (*originale originans*); that of his descendants is originated original sin (*originale originatum*). Adam's sin was personal and grave, and it affected human nature. It was personal because he freely committed it; it was grave because God imposed a serious obligation; and it affected the whole human race by depriving his progeny of the supernatural life and preternatural gifts they would have possessed on entering the world had Adam not

sinned. Original sin in his descendants is personal only in the sense that the children of Adam are each personally affected, but not personal as though they had voluntarily chosen to commit the sin; it is grave in the sense that it debars a person from the beatific vision, but not grave in condemning one to hell; and it is natural only in that all human nature, except for divine intervention, has it and can have it removed only by supernatural means.

PASCHAL MYSTERY—The title of a document, Paschalis Mysterii, issued by Pope Paul VI on May 9, 1969. In this document he approved a reorganization of the liturgical year and calendar for the Roman Rite. Its purpose was "to permit the faithful to communicate in a more intense way, through faith, hope and love, in the whole mystery of Christ, which . . . unfolds within the cycle of a year." Paschal Mystery is a general term to describe the redemptive work of Christ, especially the events of the Last Supper and the Passion, reaching their climax on Easter Sunday. (Etym. Latin *paschalis*, from *pascha*, Passover, Easter; from Greek *pasha*; from Hebrew *Pesah*, *Pesach*.)

PASSOVER—The Jewish Pasch celebrated annually as commanded by God to commemorate the deliverance of the Israelites from the bondage of Egypt. Its main feature was the sacrificial meal, ending with eating the paschal lamb, followed by the seven-day Feast of the Unleavened Bread. At the time of Christ the Passover meal united the Jewish family from sunset to midnight on the fifteenth of Nisan. Its last celebration by the Savior was the occasion for instituting the Eucharist and the priesthood of the New Law.

PENANCE—The virtue or disposition of heart by which one repents of one's own sins and is converted to God. Also the punishment by which one atones for sins committed, either by oneself or by others. And finally the sacrament of penance, where confessed sins committed after baptism are absolved by a priest in the name of God. (Etym. Latin *paenitentia*, repentance, contrition.)

PENTECOST—Feast commemorating the descent of the Holy Spirit on the Apostles. It takes its name from the fact that it comes about fifty days after Easter. The name was originally given to the Jewish Feast of Weeks, which fell in the fiftieth day after Passover, when the first fruits of the corn harvest were offered to the Lord (Deuteronomy 16:9), and, later on, the giving of the law to Moses was celebrated. In the early Church, Pentecost meant the whole period from Easter to Pentecost Sunday, during which no fasting was allowed, prayer was only made standing, and Alleluia was sung more often. (Etym. Greek *pentēkostē*, the fiftieth day.)

PROMISED LAND—The land of Canaan, generally thought to be the whole of western Palestine. It was promised to the Israelites by God after their sojourn in the desert (Exodus 12:25).

PROPHET—The biblical term "nabi" means one who spoke, acted, or wrote under the extraordinary influence of God to make known the divine counsels and will. Yet commonly associated with this primary function to proclaim the word of God, a prophet also prophesied by foretelling future events. His role, then, was to both proclaim and to make the proclamation credible.

RECONCILIATION, SACRAMENT OF—See PENANCE

RESURRECTION, BODILY—The universal return to life of all human beings, to occur soon before the last judgment by God's almighty power. Each individual soul will be reunited with the selfsame body with which it was united on earth. While all the dead will rise, only the just will have their bodies glorified.

RITE—In general, the manner and form of a religious function. Hence the words and actions to be carried out in the performance of a given act, e.g., the rite of baptism, or the rite of consecration, the Roman Rite. The term in its widest ecclesiastical sense refers to the principal historic rituals in the Catholic Church, whose essentials are the same as derived from Jesus Christ. The four parent rites in Catholicism are the Antiochene, Alexandrine, Roman, and Gallican. Some religious orders have their own rites. In all cases, however, the ritual must be approved by the Holy See. (Etym. Latin *ritus*, religious custom, usage, ceremony.)

SABBATH—The Jewish day of rest, with elaborate prescriptions for its observance. Failure to observe the Sabbath was one of the principal accusations of the Pharisees against Jesus. It began on Friday night at sundown and ended on Saturday at sundown. No manual labor was done on the Sabbath. This meant complete withdrawal from business and trade interests, and giving oneself to family, friends, and religion. On the preceptive side, the Sabbath was to intensify home life, deepen one's knowledge of religious history and religion, and above all concentrate on prayer and things of the spirit. Already in apostolic times (Acts 20:7) Christians transferred the Sabbath from the seventh to the first day of the week. Moreover, the Catholic understanding of Sunday as a Sabbath (rest) has never been as rigid as that of some Protestant groups, e.g., the Puritans.

SACRAMENT—A sensible sign, instituted by Jesus Christ, by which invisible grace and inward sanctification are communicated to the soul. The essential elements of a sacrament of the New Law are institution by Christ the God-man during his visible stay on earth, and a sensibly perceptible rite that actually confers the supernatural grace it symbolizes. In a broad sense every external sign of internal divine blessing is a sacrament. And in this sense there were already sacraments in the Old Law, such as the practice of circumcision. But, as the Council of Trent defined, these ancient rites differed essentially from the sacraments of the New Law, they did not really contain the grace they signified, nor was the fullness of grace yet available through visible channels merited and established by the Savior. (Etym. Latin *sacramentum*, oath, solemn obligation; from *sacrare*, to set apart as sacred, consecrate.)

SACRED CHRISM/SACRUM CHRISMA—See CHRISM

SANCTIFYING GRACE—The supernatural state of being infused by God, which permanently inheres in the soul. It is a vital principle of the supernatural life, as the rational soul is the vital principle of a human being's natural life. It is not a substance but a real quality that becomes part of the soul substance. Although commonly associated with the possession of the virtue of charity, sanctifying grace is yet distinct from this virtue. Charity, rather, belongs to the will, whereas sanctifying grace belongs to the whole soul, mind, will, and affections. It is called sanctifying grace because it makes holy those who possess the gift by giving them a participation in the divine life. It is *zoē* (life), which Christ taught that he has in common with the Father and which those who are in the state of grace share.

SANCTUARY LAMP—A wax candle, generally in a red glass container, kept burning day and night wherever the Blessed Sacrament is reserved in Catholic churches or chapels. It is an emblem of Christ's abiding love and a reminder to the faithful to respond with loving adoration in return.

SCAPULAR—An outer garment consisting of two strips of cloth joined across the shoulders, worn by members of certain religious orders. Originating as the working frock of Benedictines, it was adopted by other religious communities and is now considered a distinctive part of the monastic habit. It symbolizes the yoke of Christ. A scapular is worn under one's secular clothes, in abbreviated form by tertiaries associated with the religious orders. Tertiary scapulars vary in size and shape; their color corresponds to that of the monastic family. As a further development, the Church has approved some eighteen blessed scapulars as two small pieces of cloth joined by strings and worn around the neck and under the clothes. Best known are the five scapulars of: Our Lady of Mount Carmel (brown), the Passion (red), Seven Dolors (black), Immaculate Conception (blue), and the Holy Trinity (white). (Etym. Latin *scapulare*, *scapularium*, "shoulder cloak," from Latin *scapula*, shoulder.)

SEAL OF CONFESSION—The grave duty of keeping absolutely secret all sins that are told in sacramental confession and anything else that is told by the penitent and is related to the confession. It is an obligation binding in the natural law, the divine law of Christ, and in the positive law of the Church. It binds the confessor and any other person who in any way discovers what was confessed. Under no circumstances may any of this information be revealed unless the penitent freely gives permission.

SEAL OF CONFIRMATION—To establish or determine irrevocably, in the sacrament of confirmation, when a bishop anoints a person with chrism and says, "[Name], be sealed with the Gift of the Holy Spirit." Thus, by confirmation a baptized Christian becomes permanently marked as a witness of Christ and is enabled to preserve, profess, and communicate the faith even (if need be) with the price of his blood.

SIN—"A word, deed or desire in opposition to the eternal law" (St. Augustine). Sin is a deliberate transgression of a law of God, which identifies the four essentials of every sin. A law is involved, implying that there are physical laws that operate with necessity, and moral laws that can be disregarded by human beings. God is offended, so that the divine dimension is never absent from any sin. Sin is a transgression, since Catholicism holds that grace is resistible and the divine will can be disobeyed. And the transgression is deliberate, which means that a sin is committed whenever a person knows that something is contrary to the law of God and then freely does the action anyway. (Etym. Old English *synn*, *syn*, sin; Old High German *sunta*, *suntea*, perhaps to Latin *sons*, guilty.)

SPIRITUAL WORKS OF MERCY—The traditional seven forms of Christian charity in favor of the soul or spirit of one's neighbor, in contrast with the corporal works of mercy that minister to people's bodily needs. They are: converting the sinner, instructing the ignorant, counseling the doubtful, comforting the sorrowful, bearing wrongs patiently, forgiving injuries, and praying for the living and the dead. Their bases are the teaching of Christ and the practice of the Church since apostolic times.

SPOUSE (BRIDE) OF CHRIST—Primarily the Church, founded by Christ, which St. Paul elaborately describes as espoused to Christ. Also a woman who vows her chastity to God in order to be more like Christ and more intimately united with him. Among certain mystics, such as Sts. Teresa of Avila and Catherine of Siena, an extraordinary union in prayer with the Savior.

TABERNACLE—A cupboard or boxlike receptacle for the exclusive reservation of the Blessed Sacrament. In early Christian times the sacred species was reserved in the home because of possible persecution. Later dove-shaped tabernacles were suspended by chains before the altar. Nowadays tabernacles may be round or rectangular and made of wood, stone, or metal. They are covered with a veil and lined with precious metal or silk, with a corporal beneath the ciboria or other sacred vessels. According to the directive of the Holy See, since the Second Vatican Council, tabernacles are always solid and inviolable and located in the middle of the main altar or on a side altar, but always in a truly prominent place (*Eucharisticum Mysterium*, May 25, 1967, II, C). (Etym. Latin *tabernaculum*, tent, diminutive of *taberna*, hut, perhaps from Etruscan.)

TEN COMMANDMENTS—Also called the Decalogue, they are the divinely revealed precepts received by Moses on Mount Sinai. Engraved on two tablets of stone, they occur in two versions in the Bible. The earlier form (Exodus 20:1-17) differs from the later (Deuteronomy 5:6-18) in two ways. It gives a religious motive, instead of a humanitarian one, for observing the sabbath; and in prohibiting avarice, it classes a man's wife along with the rest of his possessions, instead of separately.

With the exception of forbidding graven images and statues and the precept about the Sabbath, the Ten Commandments are an expression of the natural law. More or less extensive sections of the Decalogue are found in the law of other ancient people However, the Ten Commandments excel the moral codes of other religious systems in their explicit monotheism, their doctrine of God's awesome majesty and boundless goodness, and their extension of moral obligation down to the most intimate and hidden desires of the human heart. The following is a standard Catholic expression of the Ten Commandments: 1. I, the Lord, am your God. You shall not have other gods besides me. 2. You shall not take the name of the Lord, your God, in vain. 3. Remember to keep holy the Sabbath day. 4. Honor your father and your mother. 5. You shall not kill. 6. You shall not commit adultery. 7. You shall not steal. 8. You shall not bear false witness against your neighbor. 9. You shall not covet your neighbor's wife. 10. You shall not covet anything that belongs to your neighbor.

TREE OF LIFE—A tree that stood next to the Tree of Knowledge in the middle of the Garden of Eden

(Genesis 2:9). It conferred on anyone eating its fruit the gift of immortality (Genesis 3:22).

THEOPHILUS—Possibly a government official or a person of high rank to whom Luke dedicated his Gospel. Most likely a potential convert, as may be inferred from Luke's final words in the introduction: ". . . how well founded the teaching is that you have received" (Luke 1:4). Luke also directed Theophilus' attention to the Acts of the Apostles, addressing him by name in the opening sentence (Acts 1:1). (Etym. Greek *theophilos*, beloved of God.)

TRANSUBSTANTIATION—The complete change of the substance of bread and wine into the substance of Christ's body and blood by a validly ordained priest during the consecration at Mass, so that only the accidents of bread and wine remain. While the faith behind the term itself was already believed in apostolic times, the term itself was a later development. With the Eastern Fathers before the sixth century, the favored expression was meta-ousiosis, "change of being"; the Latin tradition coined the word transubstantiatio, "change of substance," which was incorporated into the creed of the Fourth Lateran Council in 1215. The Council of Trent, in defining the "wonderful and singular conversion of the whole substance of the wine into the blood" of Christ, added "which conversion the Catholic Church calls transubstantiation" (Denzinger 1652). After transubstantiation, the accidents of bread and wine do not inhere in any subject or substance whatever. Yet they are not make-believe; they are sustained in existence by divine power. (Etym. Latin *trans-*, so as to change + *substantia*, substance: *transubstantio*, change of substance.)

TRINITY, THE HOLY—A term used since A.D. 200 to denote the central doctrine of the Christian religion. God, who is one and unique in his infinite substance or nature, is three really distinct persons, the Father, Son, and Holy Spirit. The one and only God is the Father, the Son, and the Holy Spirit. Yet God the Father is not God the Son, but generates the Son eternally, as the Son is eternally begotten. The Holy Spirit is neither the Father nor the Son, but a distinct person having the divine nature from the Father and the Son by eternal procession. The three divine persons are co-equal, co-eternal, and consubstantial and deserve co-equal glory and adoration.

VENIAL SIN—An offense against God which does not deprive the sinner of sanctifying grace. It is called venial (from *venia*, pardon) because the soul still has the vital principle that allows a cure from within, similar to the healing of a sick or diseased body whose source of animation (the soul) is still present to restore the ailing bodily function to health.

Deliberate venial sin is a disease that slackens the spiritual powers, lowers one's resistance to evil, and causes one to deviate from the path that leads to heavenly glory. Variously called "daily sins" or "light sins" or "lesser sins," they are committed under a variety of conditions: when a person transgresses with full or partial knowledge and consent to a divine law that does not oblige seriously; when one violates a law that obliges gravely but either one's knowledge or consent is not complete; or when one disobeys what is an objectively grave precept but due to invincible ignorance a person thinks the obligation is not serious.

The essence of venial sin consists in a certain disorder but does not imply complete aversion from humanity's final destiny. It is an illness of the soul rather than its supernatural death. When people commit a venial sin, they do not decisively set themselves on turning away from God, but from over fondness for some created good, fall short of God. They are like persons who loiter without leaving the way.

VIATICUM—The reception of Holy Communion when there is probable danger of death. Viaticum should not be deferred too long in sickness lest the dying lose consciousness. It can be given as often as such danger exists, and is required of all the faithful who have reached the age of discretion. No laws of fasting persist either for the recipient or for the priest who must consecrate in order to supply the Host in an emergency. (Etym. Latin *viaticum*, traveling provisions; from *viaticus*, of a road or journey, from *via*, way, road.)

VOCATION—A call from God to a distinctive state of life, in which the person can reach holiness. The Second Vatican Council made it plain that there is a "Universal call [*vocatio*] to holiness in the Church" (*Lumen Gentium*, 39). (Etym. Latin *vocatio*, a calling, summoning; from *vocare*, to call.)

VOW—A free, deliberate promise made to God to do something that is good and that is more pleasing to God than its omission would be. The one vowing must realize that a special sin is committed by violating the promise. A vow binds under pain of sin (grave or slight) according to the intention of the one taking the vow. If one vows with regard to grave matter, one is presumed to intend to bind oneself under pain of serious sin. Vows enhance the moral value of human actions on several counts. They unite the soul to God by a new bond of religion, and so the acts included under the vow become also acts of religion. Hence they are more meritorious. By taking a vow, a person surrenders to God the moral freedom of acting otherwise, like the one who not only gives at times the fruit of the tree, but gives up the tree itself. And vows forestall human weakness, since they do not leave matters to the indecision or caprice of the moment. Their very purpose is to invoke divine grace to sustain one's resolution until the vow expires or, in the case of perpetual vows, even until death. (Etym. Latin *vovere*, to pledge, promise.)

Used with permission of Inter Mirifica.

For additional definitions, please see Fr. John Hardon's *Modern Catholic Dictionary*, © 2000 Eternal Life Publications or *Catholic Dictionary: An Abridged and Updated Edition of Modern Catholic Dictionary*, © 2013 Inter Mirifica.

Sophia Institute

Sophia Institute is a nonprofit institution that seeks to nurture the spiritual, moral, and cultural life of souls and to spread the gospel of Christ in conformity with the authentic teachings of the Roman Catholic Church.

Sophia Institute Press fulfills this mission by offering translations, reprints, and new publications that afford readers a rich source of the enduring wisdom of mankind.

Sophia Institute also operates the popular online resource CatholicExchange.com. *Catholic Exchange* provides world news from a Catholic perspective as well as daily devotionals and articles that will help readers to grow in holiness and live a life consistent with the teachings of the Church.

In 2013, Sophia Institute launched Sophia Institute for Teachers to renew and rebuild Catholic culture through service to Catholic education. With the goal of nurturing the spiritual, moral, and cultural life of souls, and an abiding respect for the role and work of teachers, we strive to provide materials and programs that are at once enlightening to the mind and ennobling to the heart; faithful and complete, as well as useful and practical.

Sophia Institute gratefully recognizes the Solidarity Association for preserving and encouraging the growth of our apostolate over the course of many years. Without their generous and timely support, this book would not be in your hands.

www.SophiaInstitute.com
www.CatholicExchange.com
www.SophiaInstituteforTeachers.org